GET IN THE CAR, JANE!

GET IN THE CAR, JANE!

ADVENTURES IN THE TELEVISION WASTELAND

BILLY VAN ZANDT

Get in the Car, Jane!
Adventures in the Television Wasteland
Copyright © 2004, 2020 by Billy Van Zandt
All rights reserved

Book Design by Falcon Books

San Ramon, California

Paperback ISBN: 978-7344017-1-4
Hard Bound ISBN: 978-7344017-2-1

Published by
Van Zandt/Milmore Productions
12400 Ventura Blvd #449
Studio City, CA 91604

Website: www.vanzandtmilmore.com

PRINTED IN THE UNITED STATES OF AMERICA

OPENING CREDITS

Walker, William, and Cody — the best days of my life are because of you. I couldn't love you more or be prouder of the men you've grown up to be.

Teresa — my very own happy ending. I love this woman. Best blind date in the history of the world!

My sister Kathi — if I make you laugh, I know I'm doing something right. Thanks for your guidance, feedback, and expertise putting this book together. I couldn't ask for a better sister. (The truth is I did ask, but Ma and Dad said they were done having kids.)

My brother Steven — you actually had nothing at all to do with this book, but I'll thank you anyway. You've kept me laughing my entire life. And an extra thank-you for taking the heat years before I told Dad that I was also going into show business.

Bruce Ferber — thank you for getting this thing rolling. We've come a long way together, my friend. Readers, I highly recommend Bruce's books: Cascade Falls; Elevating Overman; and The Way We Work: On the Job in Hollywood (which contains a great chapter on Lucille Ball).

Rob Reinalda — I'm so glad we've reconnected after all these years. Winner of the 2019 ACES Robinson Prize for Excellence in Editing. What more can I say? How could I go wrong?

Rebecca Zaccarino and Dan Gilvezan — thank you for your insightful notes. (Not that I used any of them, but they were pretty damn good notes.)

Ken and Roberta at Falcon Books — I left you hanging for 14 years, but we're finally here. Sorry I took so long that Roberta retired.

Tom Chesek — thank you for your cover art. Tom's been drawing caricatures of me since junior high. A brilliant guy. I'm so glad I forced him into this. Go visit him at the Stephen Crane House in Asbury Park, New Jersey. Tell him Billy sent you.

Don Rickles — thank you for your quote, your friendship, and the thrill of a lifetime working with you.

Noel Kubel — thank you for designing the cover. Noel's been with me for most of my career. His friendship is invaluable. And so are his logos, which are seen around the world on the posters of our plays. Say hello to Prague for me.

And, of course, Lucille Ball, Desi Arnaz, Vivian Vance, William Frawley, Bob Carroll Jr., Madelyn Davis, Bob Schiller, Bob Weiskopf, and Jess Oppenheimer — for everything.

And one final, extra thank-you to my writing partner of a hundred and fifty years, Jane Milmore. I love you. And without you, the title of this book would make no sense whatsoever.

TEASER

Why are you reading this? Don't you know nobody reads anymore? That's why I thought this would be a safe time to write about my years in TV and recount things about the people I worked with — without anyone actually seeing it.

OK, that's not *entirely* true, but I have always wanted to write a book. The big question was what to write about.

Then I got a call out of the blue. My friend, the author Bruce Ferber, phoned to ask if he could use a story I'd written some years back to be part of his Hollywood anthology "The Way We Work" (Rare Bird Books). As I reread and edited my essay about working with Lucille Ball for his collection of show biz tales, I started looking at a few other papers I'd written about my time in television.

And there was my book.

This is not an autobiography. These are stories I tell about some of the television shows I've worked on. All are taken from journals.

My writing partner of a hundred and fifty years, Jane Milmore, confirms the stories and the quotes I'd recorded in my journals. And to confirm those confirmations, I also ran each chapter past people who were with me at the time of each story. Not that there are any bombshells I'm dropping, but I want to be accurate.

You'll learn the business as I learned it. Naïve at times, stupidly arrogant at other times, but always honored and thrilled to be part of it all.

If I've mentioned you in a story and you don't agree with my recollection of events, well, then, feel free to write your own book.

Mostly, this memoir is written for my sons, to finally answer the question: What do you do at the studio all day, Dad?

Here you go, guys.

Contents

I STALK LUCY

Lucille Ball and Life with Lucy

1000 N. Roxbury Drive. A white, modern colonial. Black shutters. Set on prime Beverly Hills real estate between Mr. & Mrs. Jack Benny and Mr. & Mrs. Jimmy Stewart, and across the street from Ira Gershwin, Rosemary Clooney, and Jose Ferrer.

It's the same house I've seen in magazines and on the episode of *I Love Lucy* when the show goes on location to film Lucy and Ethel sneaking across Richard Widmark's front lawn.

It's Lucille Ball's home.

It's 1977. I've flown to Hollywood to film scenes for *Jaws 2,* my first movie as an actor (soon to realize filmmaking would involve swimming in polluted waters outside a cat food cannery in Long Beach).

It's my first time here. I don't go to Grauman's Chinese Theater, Dodger Stadium, or the Hollywood Bowl. I go to Lucy's house — straight from the airport.

I pull up in front of No. 1000 in my rented Toyota and fling open the car door. Jane, my girlfriend at the time, freaks out.

"What do you think you're doing?!"

"I'm going to meet Lucy!" I say as I jump out.

Jane won't get out of the car. She buries her blonde head under the dashboard as I stride up the brick walkway to ring the bell.

Lucy is the reason I'm in show business. She taught me comic timing. Her writers taught me how to write. Desi Arnaz showed us all how to produce. And Lucy is the one who still makes me laugh more than anyone else.

The Lucy character and I more than connect. Most of the time I feel like I'm living an *I Love Lucy* episode, fearlessly jumping into one situation after another, then figuring out how things will work out after the fact.

The front door opens, and a little Japanese houseboy pops his head out.

"Yes?"

I announce myself: "Billy Van Zandt — here to see Lucille Ball."

"She's not home," he says, slamming the door in my face.

I walk back to the car, get in, grab my camera, and start snapping as Jane peels out.

* * *

Ten years later.

Sitting inside Lucy's house after watching the premiere of *Life with Lucy* with Lucy, her husband Gary Morton, Gale Gordon, John Ritter, and members of the show's cast, including my friend Ann Dusenberry.

I ask Lucy if she ever met Charlie Chaplin, since it's obvious he has influenced her. I've never seen a photo of them together nor heard they'd met.

She says: "No. But in 1976 Gary and I were in Switzerland. I found out where he lived, so Gary and I drove over. When we pulled up in front of Chaplin's house, I jumped out, but Gary hid his head under the dashboard and refused to leave the car. I left him sitting there, walked up to the front door, and rang the bell. A big fat housekeeper opened the door and asked what I wanted. I said, 'Lucille Ball — here to see Charlie Chaplin.' She said, 'He's not home,' and slammed the door in my face."

* * *

Three weeks earlier I was in New Jersey preparing to open a new theater with Jane. At the same time, we were opening the Off-Broadway production of our murder-mystery spoof, *Drop Dead!* I got a phone call that put it all on hold.

My *Jaws 2* buddy Ann Dusenberry had landed the role of Lucy's daughter on her new TV series, *Life with Lucy.* Ann told me, "After my mother, you were the first one I called."

I, of course, realized there was only one reason Lucy was coming back to TV — so I could meet her, learn from her, and ultimately work with her.

With no notice, and with Ann's permission, I leave the theater duties to Jane and jump on a plane to L.A. to watch Lucy rehearse an episode.

When I arrive, Ann tells me she's sorry, but she's been told it's a "closed set." No one can enter the soundstage during rehearsals, let alone watch. I tell her I understand. Then I sneak up to the bleachers.

I look down. There she is. A mop of orange hair. Big sunglasses.

* * *

I saw Lucy in person once before, in New York City, when she was filming the TV movie *Stone Pillow.* I was on the West Side in a meeting with Sean Penn and director Jamie Foley for *At Close Range*, a project I helped put together. In the middle of my meeting, I heard Lucy's voice booming through the heating vents. "Where's that coming from?" I asked. The casting lady explained Lucille Ball was rehearsing in the next room.

Sean, with whom I'd acted in the movie *Taps*, knew of my Lucy obsession and started laughing. He'd ridden past her house with me several times. Me, because I wanted to meet her. Sean, because he thought it was funny. Whenever someone new came to town, I'd always drive from the airport straight to Roxbury Drive. And that included when our friend Tom Cruise moved out to L.A. Yes, Lucy, that was Sean Penn, Tom Cruise, and I parked outside your house.

Back at my meeting, Sean heard Lucy's voice through the wall and motioned, "Go ahead."

Ten minutes later, wearing overalls supplied by the casting lady, I enter the *Stone Pillow* rehearsal room pretending to be an air conditioner repairman and stand next to the air conditioner unit (which is working perfectly fine) and mime pushing buttons.

My very own "Lucy Meets Billy" episode, but I don't accidentally spill something on the star or knock down a wall. I watch for five minutes and then leave before I get the casting lady fired.

* * *

That was two years earlier.

Lucy sees me in the bleachers. She leans over to say something to Ann, who whispers back. Lucy rises, walking to the edge of the bleachers and looks up.

I think: "I just got Ann fired."

And: "I'm going to get thrown out. By Lucy."

Instead, she stares at me. And in her best "It's a moo-moo" Martian-voice says, "Hello, Billy. I heard you were coming."

For the rest of the week, it's still a closed set. With one exception. Lucy plays to an audience of one. Me.

* * *

Watching her work is surreal. Lucy holds back in rehearsal, walking through, "marking" where her laughs will come. Then she runs scenes over and over. As she gets more comfortable, her confidence builds, and she gets funnier and funnier until it looks effortless.

She insists on having her exact props as soon as possible, so she has plenty of time to work out the nuances of using them — a lesson she'd learned from Buster Keaton from her years at MGM.

Lucy is all about her props.

Madelyn Davis (one of the show's producers and one of the original *I Love Lucy* writers) tells me that in the old days whenever they needed a prop for a scene, Lucy knew the Desilu props so well she could tell them where to look in the warehouse — which shelf, which row, and how many colors it came in.

From the bleachers, I watch her figure out physical bits in a mechanical way and then rehearse them until they seem spontaneous. I realize I rehearse the same way —probably a result of my watching her for 20 years, imitating her timing. It's also my belief that every comedian is born hearing a certain rhythm. I think I connect with Lucy because we both have the same ear, only she's a master and I'm still learning.

Tom Watson, Lucy's assistant and a best-selling author, comes up to me as I watch rehearsal.

"You've never seen her work before, have you?"

I ask how he could tell.

He says he could tell by the look of shock on my face when I saw her working off cue cards.

It's true. I always thought her "takes" out front were for effect, to sell the punchlines. Now I know they were to simply to read the lines. For years I've imitated her style, only I never had the cards.

During a break, I ask Lucy how long she'd been using cue cards. She tells me: "Thirty years. I was running a studio and producing 17 shows. So when did I have time to learn lines?" Despite the fact she is no longer running a studio or producing anything other than this one show, I don't feel the need to argue.

* * *

In a scene with the boy playing her grandson, Lucy — in character — keeps saying, "What?" — forcing him to talk louder. I'm told she did the same thing with Richard Burton and Elizabeth Taylor when they guest-starred on *Here's Lucy*.

"Who the hell does she think she is doing that to me?" demanded Sir Richard Burton.

To which Elizabeth Taylor answered: "The Queen of Comedy, dear."

* * *

Lucy starts one scene and, still in character, tells the gaffer which light is incorrectly focused behind her. Without missing a line, she changes an actor's blocking by dragging him by his arm while they play the scene out — silently pointing out where he should stand for a better camera angle — against the director's silent objection.

An actor starts to deliver a line while walking, apparently sacrilege to Lucy. She yells, "What the hell's the matter with you? Talk! *Then* walk!"

He doesn't do it again.

* * *

From the first day, Lucy is "on."

It's unreal to see her in person as the only audience member. It's like I'm 10 years old in my parents' living room, lying on the floor in front of the TV.

During a break, Gale Gordon tells me that Lucy must like me, because she's apparently performing for me personally.

"Normally she doesn't work this hard."

* * *

Between scenes, she tells me about filming *Room Service* with the Marx Brothers and how they spent an entire day without pants the day a busload of nuns came to visit the set. She talks about Desi Arnaz— how underappreciated he was in Hollywood, despite the fact he virtually invented the sitcom.

Lucy tells me how to time a gag: "Listen, react — and *then* act." I already know this because as a "Lucy freak" I know all the stories.

We share a Snickers bar and talk about plays I've written, which I confess are thinly disguised *Lucy* episodes with me in the male "Lucy" role.

Lucy listens, pausing, then asks whether I could do anything with "this" — indicating the script. I'm terrified to say an unkind word about the original *Lucy* writers who are producing *Life with Lucy,* so I assure her I think it's funnier than she does, probably passing up my first TV writing job in the process.

"Is it? I haven't known what's funny for 30 years. When everybody laughs at everything you do, how can you know?"

* * *

A few days into the week, Director Marc Daniels takes me aside. "Knock it off."

"What did I do?"

"She's telling you too many stories. It's making the day longer."

I go back up into the stands—where I see next week's script.

At first I think the white light on it is from heaven, but I quickly realize it's a work light.

I open the script and see two words written especially for me, right there in the cast list: "Delivery Guy."

In one scene, Lucy has messed up the hardware store's computer system so that Gale Gordon's character somehow ends up listed dead in the newspaper, and the Chamber of Commerce sends flowers to his funeral. Does it make sense? No. But who cares? The flowers have to be delivered by a delivery guy! In a scene with Lucy *and* Gale Gordon!

I run across the lot into the casting director's office — a man who has no idea who I am or why I'm standing in his office — and demand to read for the role. He's snippy, telling me: "We don't hold auditions for 'Lucy.' We only watch actors' videotapes."

"I don't have any tape with me — I'm on vacation."

"Then you're out of luck. No videotape — no audition."

With the help of Stu Shostak, Lucy's video archivist, I go to a local video store and rent my only two movies of note: *Jaws 2* and *Taps*.

We splice together an acting reel of videotape.

Two hours later I walk into the casting director's office, flinging my tape on his desk. The casting director is either amazed at my spunk or terrified that I will kill him if I don't get this audition.

He grants me an audition with Madelyn Davis and Bob Carroll Jr.

* * *

The next morning in the waiting room I look at the sign-in sheet. There is one other name up for the same role: a comedian named Arsenio Hall.

I'm called in to read first. I ask Bob and Madelyn if I can share something before I read the scene. They say yes.

And so I speak from the heart for about 10 minutes: How they've influenced me as a writer and shaped my entire life with their work. How every television writer owes them everything — for creating the rules and showing how it's supposed to be done. I don't care if I get the role or not. Nothing can stop me from thanking them.

When I'm done rambling, I read the scene for them — all four lines. They laugh. I thank them again and, thinking I've blown the audition by brown-nosing, I go back to the bleachers to watch the rest of the rehearsal.

Madelyn finds Ann and informs her she can be the one to tell me — I got the job. I love Ann a little more than I already do. That night I call Jane at our theater back in New Jersey. Over the sound of hammers and electric drills on the other end of the line, I tell her I'll be staying an extra week. I'm going to act with Lucy!

* * *

The following Monday I walk onto the soundstage. Gale Gordon comes up to me and sticks out his hand: "Welcome to the family."

The hairs on the back of my neck stand up.

* * *

We read. We rehearse. And here I am, acting with Lucy and Gale, directed by the great Marc Daniels, who has directed some of my favorite "Lucy" episodes — in a show produced by Bob and Madelyn — with a script written by Arthur Marx, the son of my other comic idol, Groucho.

I'm terrified — especially when, after the first day's rehearsal, they start cutting the script because it's too long. I panic that my meeting with destiny will be written out of the show. Instead, they move the scene intact from the hardware store set to the house set.

Phew!

The week is a blur, except for loving every second of it.

* * *

The best is when Marc Daniels tries to change something I'm doing and Lucy booms: "Leave him alone. He knows what he's doing. He's a very talented comedian."

I call Jane that night to tell her if my plane goes down on my flight home, it's OK with me. Lucy said I was talented.

* * *

Friday's opening night. We shoot the show.

It feels like a theater opening night. Everybody has butterflies. The actors and the sets are hidden from the audience by big screens. We're told we will only do each scene once — like a live play.

As we sit backstage waiting to start, Lucy, in a silly mood, goes around to each one of us and mimes that she's feeling each of us up. I have no idea why. But that's what she does. She's one of the gang.

I say, "I'd feel you up, too, but I'd feel funny feeling up an institution."

She laughs that big hearty deep laugh of hers. And the show begins.

* * *

It is an eternity waiting to get on stage, but once my cue comes, out I walk. Gale Gordon feeds me my cue, I get my quick laughs, and I exit.

As the door shuts behind me, I too loudly tell actor Donovan Scott, waiting for his own entrance, "I want to do it again!"

He shushes me. The show is still going on.

I've waited my whole life for this moment, and now it's over.

I have instant images of being the Sid Gould of the show — Gary Morton's cousin who appeared on every Here's Lucy episode as the delivery guy, the mailman, the UPS guy, whatever they needed. Not much of a goal, I admit — and one I guarantee absolutely no one on earth has ever had before or since — including Sid Gould.

After the show, Lucy thanks me for a great job. And she poses for a photo with me. A hundred flashes go off, as the fans who stayed behind in the bleachers snap photos of The Queen of Comedy.

* * *

I never knew who took those photos of Lucy and me that night, but I sure would like a copy — my autofocus camera focused only on the set behind Lucy and me. On the bright side, Lucy probably would have preferred knowing we shot a soft-focus still.

* * *

As they call the show a wrap, I ready myself for the flight back to the real world and the unfinished work I've left to Jane.

Until Lucy says, "What are you doing next Monday?"

"Nothing."

"Come over the house. I'm having a few people over to watch the first episode."

I call Jane. "One more week."

I hope the big pause before she says, "Oh, that's great," means she's thrilled for me.

* * *

Ann and I arrive at Lucy's house.

As I did 10 years earlier, I walk up the brick driveway. Only this time no houseboy opens the door. It's Lucille Ball herself — with a big stem glass in her hand filled with what looks like either a margarita or Mountain Dew.

The reviews are out, and they haven't been nice. In fact, they've been cruel.

In her best Lucy-Carmichael-with-way-too-much-to-drink voice, she pretends to stagger and slur her words as she announces herself to us at the front door: "Hello. I used to be in television!"

* * *

She gives us a quick tour of the house. It's quite beautiful and homey. Scrapbooks and photos of her kids are everywhere, and a big backgammon table sits in the corner of the room — where I'm told she has spent the last 10 years mostly drinking her "slushies" (margarita mix minus the tequila) and playing backgammon with friends until *Life with Lucy* came along.

When you're from the East Coast and you come out to Hollywood, you expect the Beverly Hills mansions to be huge *Beverly Hillbillies* mansions. The Hearst Castle. Pickfair. This is a nice big house that a well-to-do doctor back East might live in. The whole block is like that. And it fits her.

She's an East Coast hard-working Yankee girl whose first priority is her family.

John and Nancy Ritter are there. Gale Gordon. Lillian Briggs, one of Lucy's close friends, who proudly announces she has just been inducted into the Asbury Park Rock and Roll Hall of Fame in New Jersey as the only female trombone player in the history of rock and roll. I tell her my brother Steven is in the Hall of Fame, too, as a member of Bruce Springsteen's E Street Band. Lucy and Lillian have no idea who or what I'm talking about.

Lucy shows us the pool house, which is covered in pictures from her film *Mame*. I'm excited to tell her we know someone in common. Gene Saks, who directed the movie, was my father's neighbor back in Hackensack, New Jersey, when they were kids. Before I get to open my mouth, Lucy quickly tells us how choreographer "Onna White really directed that picture. Not that 'so-called' director Gene Saks." I wisely decide to keep my "someone in common" to myself.

As we leave the pool house, Lucy tells me I look like Bronson Pinchot from *Perfect Strangers*. I think she means it as a compliment. I tell her I'm much better looking. She isn't sure if I'm making a joke or not and agrees with me.

We eat spaghetti and meatballs. And Duncan Hines chocolate cake for dessert. I compliment Lucy on the food. She bows her head graciously then, pointing to the Japanese couple in the corner, announces, "Yeah, they can cook anything."

After dinner, I sit on the floor in front of the TV and watch the first network airing of *Life with Lucy*.

Halfway through the show I realize Lucy, who is sitting in the back of the room, isn't watching the TV. She's watching me watch the show. A surreal moment made more surreal.

After the show, a movie screen is lowered out of the ceiling and we watch an Eddie Bracken movie from 1944 (Preston Sturges's *Hail the Conquering Hero*). Then we all sit around listening to Lucy talk about the old days. We also hear about a famous song-and-dance man's secret closet filled with women's clothes and how his wife got a great divorce settlement when she threatened to expose it.

The topic of colorization of old black-and-white movies comes up. Finally feeling comfortable with my new friends, I give my animated opinion that it's a sin to ruin classic black-and-white films with color. Lucy nods and then, indicating her husband, deadpans, "Tell that to Gary; he's in the colorization business." I quickly tell him that must be interesting work and change the subject back to the famous song-and-dance man's dresses.

* * *

Later that night as we leave, a small group of fans has gathered on the sidewalk. The star-struck new owner of Jack Benny's house leans out her window to say hello to Lucy. It's unsettling, thinking Lucy has to endure these fans every single day — and that I'm one of them.

Lucy thanks me for my good work on the show and wishes me luck with the New Jersey theater and the New York play. I thank her for teaching me so much and showing me what I wanted to do with my life. She gives me a hug, which I don't expect, and I walk out into the night.

* * *

My bio for our show's playbill that year reads, "He worked with Lucy once."

BACK STORY

California, here we come

I've known I wanted to perform from the time I was 10 — or, according to my parents, from the age of 3½, when my little sister Kathi came home from the hospital and, as all the relatives made a big deal over the new arrival, I threw a garbage can down the stairs and demanded that someone "pay attention to me!"

Performing, to me, was doing improv shows in the backyard raising money for Jerry's Kids, or putting on puppet shows for my cousins. And always writing: plays for the neighborhood friends, plays for my grammar school and junior high classes.

I studied everybody. The Marx Brothers. Buster Keaton and Charlie Chaplin, thanks to Lillian Gish's hosting of silent movies on PBS on Friday nights. But mostly Lucy. If she's on four times a day, I watch her four times a day. Not just to laugh. But to watch the timing.

I defy anyone to ride an audience as well as she does in milking the extra laughs at the conveyor belt in the chocolate factory. Those aren't scripted laughs. And the timing of her nonchalant pose after Ricky tangos with her, smashing the eggs she has hidden under her shirt, is simply perfect.

In my teens, I run the children's theater at the nearby Barn Theater, in tony Rumson, New Jersey, writing fractured fairy tales once a week, casting them the day before and rehearsing them the mornings of the shows — a great tool for the pace of what is to come in television. They are crazy shows for kids — a series of shows about an inept super hero whose Clark Kent disguise is a big rubber nose and glasses; one that guest-stars E Street Band member Garry W. Tallent and my Aunt Addie as evil banditos who have kidnapped Santa Claus for ransom (the things you do for friends!); and two with a phenomenal drag queen we met in a local production of *Peter Pan*, who plays the role of Cinderella's stepmother as Bette Davis, and the witch in *Sleeping Beauty* as Tallulah Bankhead.

Although my parents are supportive — front row at every school show — my father thinks all people in show business are either drunks or drug addicts or bums, and he does all he can to talk me out of pursuing this as a profession. I think the worst day of his life is the day he asks me if I am trying out for the school's baseball team and I answer, no, because I'm going to be in the chorus of *Oliver!*

My junior high and high school drama teachers encourage me to go after my dreams. These names may mean nothing to you, but they mean everything to me: Lois Martineau, Laine Sutton, and Lucille Brothers.

I write my first full-length musical in junior high. *The Old Bird Sanctuary in the Park Trick (And I Fell for It)* stars, well, me as Felix T. Filibuster, doing a shameless imitation of Groucho Marx. At one point I want Felix to tango with a Margaret Dumont character and spin her backward until she falls into a working fountain. Lois Martineau doesn't bat an eye; she builds the huge fountain and puts it center stage, where it sprays water through the entire show and catches poor Laura Stannard as she is flung backward into the water. *Bird Sanctuary* has a crazy finale with Rockettes, live dogs, every teacher from my school skating around the audience in choir robes, Santa throwing candy to the kids in the audience, a snow machine, balloons falling on the audience like the end of a political convention, and an out-of-the-blue, 30-piece marching band that comes storming down the center aisle.

As you may have guessed, subtlety is not my thing.

By the time I'm in high school, I still have no clue how to become a professional actor. No one in our family is in show business. My older brother Steven is in garage bands, but all that's gotten him so far is being thrown out of the house and harassed by the Middletown police for having long hair.

Jane Milmore and I meet in a local high school acting competition. Jane is from Keansburg High School, and I'm from Middletown High School, both located in Central New Jersey. (Yes, that's a thing.)

The Barn Theater holds annual drama competitions for high schools statewide. Jane and her class do a scene from *Plaza Suite.* Our school does a scene from *Lovely Ladies, Kind Gentlemen,* the musical version of *The Teahouse of the August Moon.* We both win.

The following year, Jane and I are cast together at the Barn in *The Star-Spangled Girl* and spend the next two years touring in various productions of Neil Simon's least favorite comedy. We play everywhere. Pop-up dinner theaters are the rage, so if a restaurant has more than six feet of space somewhere, they shove a stage onto it, and in we come.

We start dating almost immediately. Then we break up. Then we date again. Then we break up. Date again. Break up. And so on. A ridiculous amount of times. People always ask why. The simple answer: We were young and stupid. Plus my mother's Italian heritage has taught me how to hold a grudge, and Jane has an Irish temper and a good arm when she's throwing a vacuum cleaner at you.

After making a name for myself in local theater, I land myself an agent in New York, who sends me on my first movie audition. "Jaws 2." (Thank you, Nancy Carson and Shirley Rich.) My four-week contract turns into an 11-month shoot and brings me friends for life and enough money to survive being an actor for a few years.

By the late '70s, Jane's and my acting careers aren't exactly flourishing as we'd hoped. I've done a few films and a lot of dinner theater — if it has "sex" in the title or at some point in the show someone is wearing boxer shorts, I've probably done it. Jane has done a few commercials and guest spots on TV. But no one is breaking down our doors to star us in anything.

I'm told by my agent, and plenty of directors, that I am hard to sell because I'm not a "type." I'm half-Italian, but up against 100% Italians for a role, I look like a WASP. WASP role? Look too ethnic. Jewish roles? WASP. I realize I have to create my own roles.

Especially when I'm cast as an alien in the first *Star Trek* movie for the legendary Robert Wise (director of *The Sound of Music,* editor of *Citizen Kane*). As happy as I am to be here, I know this can't lead anywhere, except to a framed photo that sits on my brother's piano so when people are horrified by this misshapen-headed freak in the frame he can say, "Oh, him? That's my brother."

So between takes of me pushing buttons on the bridge as an alien and being forbidden to leave the Paramount lot for lunch because of the secrecy of the film and my elaborate makeup, Jane and I barricade ourselves in my dressing room and write a play to star ourselves in. Well, mostly me.

Love, Sex, and the I.R.S. is an old-fashioned farce about two roommates trying to pull a con on an I.R.S. investigator. Frankly, it's a Lucy episode — with me in the Lucy role, with the role of the mother written specifically for Vivian Vance, should I ever get to meet her.

In writing the play, I use all the things the *I Love Lucy* writers taught me through their shows. How to structure. How to leave seeds along the way that pay off in the final act. How to start slow and build to a crazy pace by the end. With room for lots of physical comedy.

Our friends Kathy Reed and Denis Lynch run The Dam Site Dinner Theater in New Jersey and agree to produce our play. The show is so successful that after being held over for a good while it comes to the attention of the country's leading play publisher, Samuel French Inc. They publish it worldwide, and it becomes a staple in summer stock with productions all around the world. That play leads to a second show and a third show, and before we know it, we're playwrights —

with 25 plays and counting as of this writing, as well as a 40-plus year tradition of writing and producing an original play every year back in our home state between TV gigs (plus a few revivals).

In 1988 our theater is sold and our Off-Broadway show *Drop Dead!* closes. After receiving a review of our play *Having a Wonderful Time, Wish You Were Her,* which said, "These people should be writing for television," we decide to move to Los Angeles and get into TV full-time, despite the fact we have no idea what we are doing.

Our plays get us an agent, who then proceeds to tell us that no one in Hollywood cares about our plays. What we need to break into television is a spec script — a great spec script.

We have no idea what that means.

He explains a spec script is simply a TV script you write on speculation (i.e., nobody pays you to do it). It not only has to be true to the show you're writing, it has to have a great story. Great jokes. Great "blows" to end each scene. And most of all, it must be better than every other spec script that's out there. It's your only calling card–and people will read you one time only. If your second spec script is funnier than your first, you're too late. The show runners who are hiring have already decided you're only as good as the one they've already read.

We're told to write a *Head of the Class* episode, which we do over the next three weeks. It is probably the best *Head of the Class* script *Head of the Class* will ever see. There is only one problem. Aside from crushing on actress Khrystyne Haje from that show, it isn't one of my all-time favorite comedies. Shows like *The Dick Van Dyke Show, The Honeymooners, Green Acres, Police Squad, Get Smart, The Mary Tyler Moore Show, The Bob Newhart Show, All in the Family, Maude,* and *I Love Lucy* are my speed. Our agent reads the *Head of the Class* script and says, "It's OK, but it didn't make me laugh much."

That's all we need to hear. Screw him!

We go home to our little apartment across from the Magic Castle in Hollywood, too naïve to realize we're living next door to a boarding house full of hookers and drug addicts, and write a scathingly funny, outrageous script for a current show we love — *Slap Maxwell* — a dark Dabney Coleman comedy about a guy going through a midlife crisis. We write it in 24 hours purely as an FU to our agent. We hand it to him the next afternoon, saying, "So, you didn't think we were funny, eh?"

Our script stays true to the show but is "out there," with Coleman's character eventually out on a ledge trying to save somebody's life and the jumper eventually taking his own life as Coleman drones on about his own miserable existence.

Our agent reads it in front of us, looks up and says, "You'll be making six figures within six months."

Within three weeks we get two offers.

And Jane and I break up again.

HIDE THE CHAIRS, MARY FRANN IS COMING!

My television debut with Newhart

We're offered two jobs — the new *Murphy Brown* and the eighth season of *Newhart*. *Newhart* received a 22-episode order. *Murphy Brown's* debut order is only for 13. We take 22 episodes.

* * *

I call my acting agent and get her machine — again.

"Maggie, the '*Newhart*' show wants to hire me as a staff writer. Please call me to discuss; I'm not sure if this is a smart move. I don't want to take this if it's going to hurt my acting career."

Three weeks later my call still hasn't been returned. I mail a postcard that says "Greetings from Hollywood" on the front, with a plea to return my call on the back.

No call.

I guess this won't hurt my acting career.

* * *

A month earlier, I had auditioned for *Newhart* and was treated like every other actor — badly. Sitting in a cramped waiting room, having parked on the street and having walked two miles to the studio lot in 100-degree heat, I ask for water and am told, "Feel free to go into the men's room and stick your head under the faucet."

Now I'm here as a writer: A nice daily drive to the lot through the guard gate, turning at the *Gilligan's Island* lagoon, driving past Beaver Cleaver's house before I park in my designated space next to the *Newhart* soundstage, two feet from my private office, complete with personalized stationery and a brand new computer. "Can we get you a drink, Mr. Van Zandt?"

The acting career can wait.

* * *

Our first two weeks of work consist of watching *Newhart* — the first seven seasons — to learn each character inside and out and see each actor's strengths. In case there's an idea for a storyline, we have to make sure it hasn't already been done.

It's odd to see early episodes. The first season was shot on videotape, and Mr. Newhart looks older eight years ago on the videotape than he does today on film.

The original show had a simple, believable premise: A man and woman open a Vermont bed-and-breakfast. Over the years, adding "Larry, Darryl, and Darryl," among other nut-job local characters, the show has evolved (or devolved) into *Green Acres.* I'm sure Barry Kemp, *Newhart's* creator who left the show to create *Coach*, must be horrified at what the succeeding executive producers did with his baby. I, however, love *Green Acres.*

My bosses are a writing team known as Mark & Mark. We hit if off instantly. They are from the East Coast and are theater lovers. They learned the process of running TV shows under my *Lucy* idols Madelyn Davis and Bob Carroll Jr. on the long-running series *Alice.* I look forward to learning from them.

* * *

All the different job titles are strange. "Staff Writer," "Story Editor," "Story Consultant," "Co-producer," "Supervising Producer," "Executive Producer" — they're all different names for "writers."

* * *

A network TV writer's season starts in early June. In "pre-production," we create the season's storylines, get studio and network approvals, and write as many scripts as we can before production starts in August.

* * *

We get one week to write a 10-page, double-spaced script outline for each script; then the producers give us detailed notes on what to change, and we get two more weeks to write a first draft. When the first draft is finished, we get more notes and an additional week to write a second draft.

After writing two-hour plays, a 22-minute script is a breeze. We write our scripts in two days and spend the rest of the time playing H-O-R-S-E on the newly installed basketball court outside the production office door.

When the second drafts are done, writers gather in the producers' spacious office and sit on couches, facing the Executive Producers at their partner desk. A writer's assistant sits on the floor with yellow legal pads to note all the changes as we go through each script line by line, with every writer on the staff getting to put in his/her two cents and the writer's assistants scribbling madly on various pads as we speak, and somehow knowing which lines are to be used and which are trash.

It's an odd adjustment for me. As playwrights, whatever Jane and I write is usually etched in stone until the audience tells us differently. Here a script is a blueprint. Arbitrary things get changed. "Hi" becomes "hello." Why? Who knows? I know if they'd leave our stuff alone it would be funnier, but it's not my show. Everything they change cuts me to the bone. I have to learn to bite my tongue. I quickly learn Writers' Room Rules:

1. Unless you have a fix for something in the script that doesn't work, keep your mouth closed.

2. If you have a fix on page 4, and we're already on page 5, keep your mouth closed.

3. If your joke is better than the one the Executive Producer decides to put in the script, keep your mouth closed.

* * *

The actors and full crew arrive at the studio in August. With the show in its eighth season, it's clear this is one big happy family. Everybody's nice. And fun. My favorite is Ellen, the script supervisor. We hit it off immediately, and she takes my love of hiking to a new height. Literally. Every weekend we go off somewhere and hike mountain trails that I'm too out of shape to admit are out of my league.

The script supervisor is in charge of continuity as you film each episode, plus meticulously timing the length of the scripts and each take that you film. I knew she'd be good at her job the first time we went hiking and she told me to meet her at the trailhead at 9:27.

We shoot three shows in a row on a Monday-to-Friday schedule. Every three weeks, the actors get a week off and the writers take the "downtime" to get more scripts ready.

On Mondays, we hold a read-through at 10 a.m. Afterward, actors get the rest of the day off. Bob Newhart literally holds his car keys in his hand as he reads, then he and actor Tom Poston go play golf at the Bel Air Country Club with comedian Dick Martin (from *Rowan & Martin's Laugh-In*), who occasionally directs for us. Then the writers go back to the Writers' Room to fix any jokes that didn't work, or trim lines if the show reads longer than our allotted 22 minutes.

We always seem to finish before 5 p.m. We're told most shows do rewrites until 2 in the morning, but our execs learned under Madelyn Davis and Bob Carroll Jr. that if you can't do the job by 5 p.m., you can't be very good.

Tuesdays and Wednesdays we work from 10 to 5. We rewrite upcoming scripts until 3, and then we go to the soundstage next door to watch the actors do a run-through. Julia Duffy and Peter Scolari always have their lines memorized. Mr. Newhart reads from the script. The run-through is done on the actual sets, which stand in a row in front of audience bleachers. We sit on director's chairs 10 feet from the actors and watch the show, marking our scripts with check marks to note a strong laugh that should be left alone, or X's to mark something that needs to be rewritten.

After each scene, our producers will alter a line or a piece of movement on the spot to fix it. Then we move on to the next scene doing the same thing.

Occasionally, Mr. Newhart gives us notes, which are always giving and supportive of the other actors:

"That joke would be better coming from Peter."

"You don't need me in that scene."

"Give Julia more in that scene."

I ask him why he's so giving. He laughs and says, "The better the show, the better I look."

* * *

After Tuesday and Wednesday run-throughs, the writers go back to the Writers' Room and compare notes, pitching jokes to replace the inferior ones that we've marked and suggesting trims if Ellen says the show is too long. Because our producers prepare the scripts so well, we change next to nothing, never working past 5 on these days, either.

* * *

Thursday is camera-blocking day. On the soundstage, the actors and the cameramen run through the show "blocking" the camera movement so on show night everything will run smoothly. The writers never go to the stage on Thursdays, because we've already locked the script from Wednesday night changes, and there's nothing for us to do. Mr. Newhart's motto is, "You've had six weeks to work on these scripts; give us two full days without making changes so we can work on them, too." He also refuses to let the show use a laugh track. "If a joke bombs, it deserves to bomb." We spend Thursdays getting ahead with other scripts.

* * *

Fridays are shoot nights. During the day we pre-shoot any scene with backwoodsmen Larry, Darryl, and Darryl, which frees up the cameras for different angles at the night-time shoot. It's odd to watch the "pre-shoots" because only Larry, Darryl, and Darryl are in costume. Otherwise everything will be shot live in front of the audience. One take, straight through, like a play.

We break for dinner, which is served in the commissary two buildings down from the stage, and then we return to the soundstage for "show night."

The younger writers sit in the bleachers to watch the show with the rest of the audience and are instructed to laugh where necessary to ensure a good audience for the actors. There are always celebrities in the audience — friends of Mr. Newhart. Natalie Schafer, who played Lovey Howell on *Gilligan's Island* sits on one side of us, and Eva Gabor from *Green Acres* on the other. I'm not sure what she's been through in the past, but Ms. Gabor is sitting with a stun gun on her lap.

Before each show begins, Mr. Newhart comes out with a microphone, welcomes the audience and introduces the actors, then performs one of his classic stand-up "telephone" routines for about 10 minutes.

What a treat to watch these private shows. (The only joke I ever see him miss with is minutes after a horrific earthquake in Armenia, as the news still shows bodies being pulled from the rubble, Mr. Newhart jokes that the worst part of the earthquake is "all the VCRs flashing: 12:00! 12:00! 12:00!")

A band plays jazz between scenes while actors change costumes and cameras reset positions. Stand-up comic JJ Wall jokes with the audience to keep things moving along. Peter Scolari even juggles to keep the audience up between scenes. A great talent in his own right, Peter's co-star from *Bosom Buddies* (a Mr. Tom Hanks) has a film career that continues to overshadow Peter. At every taping, someone in the audience inevitably asks if he's heard from Tom Hanks — and then asks, "Why does Tom do movies and you're still just on TV?"

* * *

On shoot night we start at 7, filming each scene once, like we're doing a live play. It's as exciting as any theater's opening night. Because we use film cameras, there's no way to know what we've shot until the editor gets the footage and goes to work. Luckily, the camera crew is terrific, and the producer says that in the seven years they've been doing it this way, they've had to reshoot a scene only once because of a missed camera angle.

Most sitcoms film from 7 p.m. until midnight. Our shoot lasts only 90 minutes from start to finish. Mr. Newhart has a standing 9 p.m. reservation at Le Cirque down the street, and we're told, "He'd better make the reservation."

After filming ends, actors are handed the script for Monday's table-read as they leave for the night, and we start all over again the following week.

"This runs so incredibly smooth." I say to our Exec Producer. "The star always sets the tone of a show. And Bob's the greatest." Yes, he is. Newhart is one big family, and it's clearly because of our star. What an honor to be here.

* * *

For a child of TV who spent each week circling the shows I wanted to watch in that week's *TV Guide,* I'm a kid in a candy store. We get to work with so many people I've loved growing up: Bob Newhart and

Tom Poston, of course, as well as Don Rickles, Johnny Carson, Tim Conway (*The Carol Burnett Show*), Bob Elliot (of Bob & Ray), Dick Martin (*Laugh-In* and *The Lucy Show*), Eileen Brennan (*Private Benjamin*), Ann Morgan Guilbert (*The Dick Van Dyke Show*), Peter Bonerz (*The Bob Newhart Show*), Elinor Donahue (*Father Knows Best*), Merv Griffin, Ed McMahon (*The Tonight Show*), comedian-turned-director David Steinberg, and my favorite — Alvy Moore, who played Hank Kimball on *Green Acres*. And who portrayed for us, well, basically, Hank Kimball from *Green Acres*.

* * *

In the first script Jane and I write for television, Julia Duffy's character falls in love with an earthy stonemason. She uncharacteristically enters pushing his wheelbarrow and the audience howls. Eight years of setup with her character as an ice princess who would never get her hands dirty, and we get the free laugh. That's one great difference from writing plays. No exposition. It's all done by the time the opening credits are through.

* * *

Mr. Newhart doesn't like being touched. His series-wife Mary Frann, on the other hand, loves to touch. We write a show where their characters (Dick and Joanne Loudon) fight, go to a therapist, and then make up at the end of the episode. At the run-through, we see the director has blocked Joanne to embrace and kiss her husband on the final line. Before any notes can be given, Bob casually walks behind us and whispers under his breath, like a little kid: "Don't let her touch me. Don't let her touch me."

Mark & Mark rise and start to give notes, and they have to think of creative ways to explain to Mary why she should stand 40 feet away from her husband when they make up at the end of the show.

"It's much more effective with a look. Much more."

* * *

Mary Frann's breasts keep growing as the season progresses. And it's not from something she's eating, because she only eats tea. At one of the run-throughs I swear there are three layers of breasts underneath her sweater. Unconsciously, I draw them on my script, trying to make sense of what I'm seeing, and once we're back in the Writers' Room I'm ashamed to admit what I did until I realize every other writer (men and women) did the exact same thing.

* * *

Mary always wants to talk — could not be friendlier — but she never stops. We get a call from the stage, "Mary Frann wants to talk to the writers." Our producer hangs up the phone. "Quick. Hide the chairs. Mary Frann is coming."

People start pushing office chairs into the bathroom.

"What are you doing?"

"If she can't sit down, she won't stay long."

In go four office chairs. There is a knock on the door.

"Nobody offer her a seat."

"But…"

"Just don't!" Mary enters the room of writers.

"Hi, Mary. What can we do for you?"

She looks around for a chair, sees none, and realizes no one's about to offer her a chair. "I just wanted to say, we haven't had a chance to talk in depth about my character. Please, don't feel restricted with me. Feel free to write me big jokes and crazy slapstick stuff. I'd love to do some real crazy *Lucy* stuff." She's quickly thanked for coming in, and, after an awkward silence, Mary leaves.

We've heard that the editors call Mary "The Wall." Because the show gets laugh after laugh after laugh, and then Mary enters, and "the comedy hits the wall."

* * *

Grateful that she came to them and wanting to make nice, our producers suggest we write Mary a pie-eating contest scene in the upcoming County Fair show. Mary will finally get to do her zany "*Lucy*" stuff." I'm not sure what makes eating pie "*Lucy* stuff," but OK. By the time it's shot, Mary has requested to wear a wig so her real hair won't get messed up, and she's eating the pies with a knife and fork, because she doesn't want to smear her makeup. The comedy "hits the wall," and it's the last "*Lucy*" bit we give her.

* * *

Tom Poston is my favorite person to write for. Even his straight lines get laughs. He must be the happiest man in show business: great job, great wife, lots of golf, and a new joke every morning. Here are the first words Tom said to me when we were introduced on Day One. Not "hello." Not "nice to meet you." This:

> "A man walks into a doctor's office. 'Doctor, you have to help me. My wife has the biggest vagina in the world.' The doctor says, 'Oh, come on. How big can it be?' The man says, 'I'll show you.' And he takes his hands and mimes a small opening with them. The doctor looks at the man's hands and says, 'Son, I hate to tell you, but that's not a very big vagina.' The man says, 'No, that's her asshole.' (Then indicating the massive, gaping space between his elbows:) 'This. This is her vagina.'"

* * *

I'm finding out you never know why changes get made in a TV show. Out of the blue, it's decided to eliminate a recurring character from seasons one through seven because his voice irritates one of our producers. So they kill the poor guy off in a script — one the actor in question is not part of.

When one character asks another for driving directions, he's told to take "The Harley Memorial Bridge." If the unsuspecting actor happened to be watching that episode when it aired, he'd learn from that one line that his character was dead and never coming back to the show. Apparently the Harley Memorial was a one-way bridge.

* * *

After working three-quarters of the season, I swear Bob Newhart has no idea who I am. Jane tells me I'm crazy. I begin to think she's right. And then Bob sits next to me at one of the run-throughs and strikes up a conversation.

"Hi."

"Hello."

"I saw your father at Marvin Davis's house yesterday."

"Who?"

"Your father."

"At whose house?"

"Marvin Davis."

"My father's never met Marvin Davis. He lives in New Jersey."

"Oh."

Bob gets up and walks away. I see him sit next to comedian Steve Allen's son Bill, head of the CBS Radford Studio where we shoot the show.

"I saw your father at Marvin Davis's house yesterday..."

* * *

Mary can't seem to change her clothes quickly enough on show nights. Changing her clothes messes up her hair and make-up so we (and the audience) sit waiting on Mary for 15 minutes at a time. Somehow Julia Duffy can change her clothes, fix her hair, touch up her makeup, and be back on the set in about 30 seconds.

After a few weeks (or maybe years) of this, Bob goes into Mary's dressing room. Ever conscious of the audience, Bob holds up the script binder that says Newhart on the front and says: "See the name of the show? Anyone can play the wife. Start changing your clothes faster."

We find an alternative. We write shows that all take place in one day, so there are zero costume changes to deal with. In one show, "Joanne" gets a real estate license, sells a house, and closes escrow all in the same afternoon, so she's able to stay in a yellow blazer the whole episode without changing her clothes.

It's ludicrous, but Mr. Newhart makes his 9 o'clock reservation.

* * *

One of my idols, Don Rickles, is guest-starring on the show, and Jane and I get to write the episode. They pay to fly Jane and me to Vegas to watch his act so we'll "be able to write a better script." They fly us first class. An incontinent old man sits across the aisle from me, and I make a mental note never to sit in the right-hand, Row 2, aisle seat on this airline ever again.

They put Jane and me up in a palatial suite; the staff treat us like royalty and escort us to ringside seats. I have never laughed so hard at anyone in my life. As we fly back to Los Angeles, I think, "This TV business is OK with me."

* * *

TV Guide singles out Jane's and my first script in the "Outstanding Things to Watch" section. It's an honor. They even mention Jane and me by name. On our first script!

We come in to work, and one of the producers catches us.

"Lay low."

"What?"

"Mark & Mark are pissed off that you got singled out. Don't open your mouth in the room today."

"Why would they care? We're all on the same show."

"Trust me. Just shut up."

In the Writers' Room, I ignore the advice and start pitching jokes on a script we're all working on. I'm instantly turned on. The joke is made fun of, the way I said it, and — surprise — they trash the *TV*

Guide blurb. For the rest of the day I just shut up. I feel like Jane. She doesn't pitch jokes in the room. She whispers them to one of us other writers, and we pitch them. When she pitches them herself, they get shot down for some reason. But when we pitch the exact same jokes they go into the script.

An uncomfortable moment in the Writers' Room that we staff writers find hilarious is when one exec's wife calls. Twice a day we sit there in complete silence and hear him whisper baby talk to his wife, while his partner's head turns red and appears about to explode waiting for the call to end so we can get back to the script.

"Oh, hi, honey. … Nothing. Writing."

"No, you can't be in next week's episode… "

"Yes, you dance, but you don't roller-skate, and we need … Not in one week, you can't! … OK … I'll talk to them."

His partner's forehead is about to bleed from the thumb tracks. The rest of us are stone silent.

"Oh, really? Just the gas bill, huh?"

Now things start to bang loudly on his partner's desk.

"I have to go. Love you, too."

* * *

It's hard to be funny in the Writers' Room, knowing we aren't supposed to talk unless it's to pitch a joke. Plus, we have to ask permission to leave the room to use the bathroom. It doesn't feel conducive to hilarity. But they've been doing this longer than I have. The scripts are great. And we do get out by 5, which gives Jane and me evenings to write our plays.

* * *

One morning before Christmas break, the producers run to each writer's office with an incredible surprise. MTM Studios gave them each $50,000 bonuses. They're ecstatic and giddy as they shove the checks under our noses.

"Can you believe this?"

Jane keeps looking out the window for a messenger to bring us something. No one ever does.

Later that same day, the writing staff is summoned to the Writers' Room. I tell Jane, "They must want to give us bonuses, too!"

We settle in, and our bosses say: "It's Christmastime and, well, it's customary on every show that the writers chip in to buy the actors and the crew gifts. So, each of you should expect to give about $300 dollars apiece."

"Huh?"

* * *

The producers love that Jane and I are actors. Every Monday we read the smaller guest-star roles at the table-read. Then actors are hired for three-day workweeks instead of five, saving the company money. Every weekend we get phone calls: "Jane, you're playing the nurse at the read-through. And sell it. If it bombs and we have to cut it, it'll be your fault."

Legendary comedian David Steinberg, who is directing this week's episode, corners Jane and me. "You should be getting paid for that, you know." I tell him we don't mind. We're having a ball. And it's a way to keep our hand in until the season ends and we can go back to our acting careers. David says, "You should still be getting paid. See? This is why you need a Jew on every show."

In the episode where Peter Scolari checks into a mental hospital, we write a role for a man who thinks he's Frank Sinatra. The producers want to use this Sinatra impersonator who apparently does such a bad impression it's ridiculous. The man can't be at the table-read (otherwise they'd have to pay him for the whole week), so they ask me to do his role. After the read-through Mr. Newhart says, "Why don't you just let Billy do it? He's hilarious."

He's told (within my earshot): "No, we have someone better coming in."

Mr. Newhart doesn't let it rest and mentions that it would be nice if Jane and I got to do something on camera before the end of the season to repay us for all the work we've done throughout the season.

He's assured. "I promise. They'll be on the show before the season ends."

Roles that I can play come and go one after another. The Sinatra impersonator they hired was so bad his role was cut down to a sight gag.

Jane gets the role of a Julia Duffy lookalike, after she's made to read the role at the table — and then audition four additional times after that.

In the season's last episode, I'm asked to come to the recording booth to voice the one-line squawking of a parrot. As I leave the soundstage, our show runner proudly says: "See? Told you we'd get you on the show!"

Working with Bob Newhart was a cruel way to start. Nothing's been that easy since.

ASSHOLE, ACTOR, SAME THING

Richard Lewis, Jamie Lee Curtis, and Anything But Love

From the eighth season of the well-oiled machine known as *Newhart*, we journey to uncharted territory — a new show called *Anything But Love*. ABL stars *Halloween's* Jamie Lee Curtis and "King of the Neurotics" comedian Richard Lewis as "Hannah" and "Marty," a novice writer and her mentor, working side by side at a Chicago magazine and obviously in love with each other, but keeping their professional heads about them in an effort to keep their friendship strong.

The best part of the gig? In addition to being full-time members of the writing staff, Jane and I are offered small roles as "Harold" and "Kelly," the office nerds. This is an unheard-of coup. I couldn't be happier.

* * *

Richard Lewis's rambling-neurotic speeches are fun to write. Richard has a weird way of working. Instead of trusting that he's learned his lines, each week Richard painstakingly Xeroxes his script in a smaller font, and then cuts out the dialogue and strategically tapes them to every prop on the set. He has words inside coffee cups, on his computer screen, on his memo pad, on pens — cheat sheets. He's like the Marlon Brando of sitcoms.

To his credit, Richard's fishing for his words only helps his character's delivery. Some of his best pauses for comic timing are actually a result of desperately trying to find his coffee cup to read the rest of the line.

* * *

Jamie Lee Curtis is a sweetheart. And wild. She's simply crazy – in a good way. So much fun. And she works her ass off. And when the press comes around she works like a seal. Spontaneously rolling around on the floor with a ball, barking, as a confused photographer snaps pictures for *People* — unsure whether what she's doing is supposed to be funny or if she's nuts. Jamie will do anything to give the press what they want, while Richard simply looks embarrassed when she starts doing these "bits." Luckily, his discomfort only makes him funnier.

Jamie's only problem as a comedienne is that she smiles at every punchline we give her, unaware she's telegraphing that she's trying to be funny. The show runner, Peter Noah, can't get her to stop it. So we simply stop writing her jokes. Now she's funny out of character-driven dialogue only — as it should be — and the telegraphing smiles have stopped.

She also has the foulest mouth I've ever heard. And I work with Jane Milmore.

"Fuck me blue!" Jamie screams at the top of her lungs if she makes a mistake in front of the studio audience. I'm mortified every time she does it. Hearing a star use foul language in front of an audience is shocking to me.

Tom Poston's "big vagina" joke on *Newhart* was jarring enough.

* * *

When we aren't rehearsing on stage, we're back in the Writers' Room working on scripts. One writer thinks it's funny to refer to actors as "assholes" in front of Jane and me. As in, "What did the 'assholes' on the stage have to say while you were down there? I mean 'actors.' Well… Actors, assholes. Same thing. Sorry, Billy and Jane."

* * *

Unlike *Newhart*, on show night the writers stand around the cameras "on the floor" in front of the audience bleachers. If a joke bombs, we scribble together alternative jokes right on the spot, and the actors jump right in and re-shoot the scene. Every scene is shot at least twice. I ask Peter why. It makes the night drag on, depletes the audience's energy, and gets the actors tired by the final scenes.

"The actors are better on the second take."

I think maybe that's because he *gives* them a second take, but OK.

* * *

Ann Magnuson has never done television. I know her from the movie *Making Mr. Right* with John Malkovich and *The Hunger* with David Bowie and Catherine Deneuve and the band Bongwater. But I'm told she is primarily known for her work as a performance artist — where, apparently, she stabbed an ALF doll and stood in an elevator listening to Muzak while she tapped the bottoms of her feet with her hands.

I have no idea what they're talking about. I've never seen performance art. Peter explains it this way: "A monologist is a stand-up comedian who can't get laughs. And a performance artist is a monologist who can't sell tickets."

On our show, Ann plays Jamie's boss, "Catherine" — hip, stressed out, and overbearing.

A table-read is the first time the script is read out loud. It tells the writers what works and what doesn't work. It tells the director where he'll need to help the actors. It gives the studio and the network a chance to "fix" things.

Ann doesn't know any of that. She eats bagels and reads the newspaper while she reads, actually stuffing food into her mouth right before she has to speak her lines. As a result, everything she says in the script dies. To the network this proves she isn't any good. To us it proves she must hate the script and this is her way to give a big "screw you" to the writers.

The next day I'm on the set. Ann asks me, "What happened to those great jokes in the first scene?"

"We cut them," I say. "They didn't get laughs."

She answers: "How could they? I was eating."

A bell goes off in her head. "Oh. If I screw it up on Monday, it comes out on Tuesday?"

"Yes, that's generally how it works."

She hasn't eaten a bagel at a table-read since.

* * *

At the first six tapings, no one in the studio audience laughs at Ann. There's been more talk from the studio and network of replacing her, but Peter keeps fighting them off.

Then the show airs. Ann's performance (played to the camera, not the studio audience) registers with the people at home. Everybody "gets" Catherine. The nuances are huge when seen on the screen. She's brilliant.

The next night we shoot another episode. This time, the studio audience laughs at everything she does. It's the same performance she gave in the first six shows. The network and the studio suddenly find her hilarious.

The power of the camera.

* * *

On day one, Richard Frank, who plays Catherine's hilarious lackey assistant "Jules," starts out on the wrong foot. He won't take a note Peter gives, getting snippy and nasty about the "sitcom-y" writing. After Peter has me demonstrate the bit he wants, for three minutes or so I think I'm about to get promoted into the role of Jules. Instead, Peter makes it clear who's in charge and who can be replaced, and Mr. Frank immediately falls into line — where he remains for the rest of the series run.

* * *

Joe Maher — an accomplished London stage actor who does a great Ringo Starr impression and an even better Maggie Smith impression — plays a well-respected theater snob whose career has waned reducing him to writing about television. We refer to him as "the comedy gun," because he can point a joke anywhere and always hit the target.

In one episode, Joe's character "Brian" is forced to interview one inane TV actor after another. The gag is that each interviewee is more degrading than the previous one. At one point Brian interviews a dimwitted starlet, then a Gary Coleman-type child actor, and finally a chimpanzee.

Peter walks into the Writers' Room with a memo. His face is bright red, and he keeps shaking his head. We ask what's wrong, and he waves a memo in the air.

"The note from the network reads, 'Should we really have Brian interview a little black boy AND a chimpanzee?'"

The whole sequence immediately ceases to be funny. We change our chimpanzee into a kangaroo (not to follow the note, but to try and get the stink out of the whole thing for ourselves). Now the joke is supposed to be Hannah telling Joe Maher's character Brian: "Your three o'clock is here." And then a kangaroo bounces in.

It's discovered that kangaroos don't jump unless they're frightened. Jamie refuses to let anyone frighten the animal, so our kangaroo sits in its cage until the cue line and then crawls onto the set — a huge, smelly kangaroo, its tail covered in feces and looking like a mutated, large rat from a 1950s sci-fi movie.

The unfunny footage of the rat-kangaroo never makes it into the edited show. And, happily, due to a sexual harassment suit, the racist exec who thought chimpanzees and black kids are the same joke, is fired. For all I know, he's replaced by a chimpanzee.

* * *

My favorite is Holly Fulger, who plays Hannah's best friend and landlady, "Robin." Holly is funny and quirky and beautiful and very Annie Hall. She's crazily unaware of the depth of her talent, which makes her even better. I love writing for her.

* * *

This Writers' Room is fun. The staff is amazing. Usually you have some people who are good joke writers. Some are great first draft writers. Some who are better with story structure. Some people that relate in one way or another to a character in the show, or the city or profession you're writing for. This staff has everything you need in each writer. And I love being in a room with people who are better than we are. We're stepping up our game.

Janis Hirsch is a riot to be around, with a gossipy, dark sense of humor that I love. She is responsible for the running joke of Hannah and Robin calling each other "Mrs. Schmenkman." Both characters imagine being married one day to the perfect man, dubbed "Mr. Schmenkman," so they call each other "Mrs. Schmenkman." Why? I have no idea. It's a bit I don't understand and don't find terribly funny. But people who love the show talk about it all the time, so I'm clearly ignorant.

* * *

My other favorite person on the show is Alan Kirschenbaum, with his Borscht Belt-comic delivery. He's what I imagine working with Mel Brooks must have been like on *Your Show of Shows*.

Some writers mumble their joke pitches before saying them out loud to the room, as they work out the joke in their heads. Alan is one of them. I continually make a fool out of him by hearing him mumble a joke that stinks and telling him, "That's good. Pitch it. *Pitch it.*"

Then I watch as he pitches his lousy joke out loud and it dies a miserable death. Then we all laugh at him as loud as we can. He falls for it every time.

What makes me laugh so hard I cry is when someone's script tanks at the table. On one occasion, we're all back in the room rewriting an episode. Alan makes a quiet quip to Jane about how lousy the script is. They don't want the writer to see them laughing at his misfortune, so Jane hides her face with her script. Alan hides *his* face with *his* script — unaware that he has scribbled across the back cover, "THIS SCRIPT SUCKS."

* * *

Mike Saltzman, another great writer, is new and a little gullible. Jamie Lee's husband (comedian/director/writer Christopher Guest) shows up to watch a taping, and he arbitrarily orders Mike to go get him a sandwich. Mike explains he's not a gopher — he's a writer. Chris Guest ignores his answer and asks for chips to go with the sandwich. Later in the taping when we need to fix a joke, Mike is nowhere to be found. He's running around trying to find a sandwich shop near the studio still open at 8 p.m.

* * *

Bruce Rasmussen, who may be the best writer I've ever worked with, is strangely quiet in the Writers' Room. But give him a computer, a dark room, and a white noise machine, and he can transform blank pages into brilliance. The running joke about Bruce is that he is always left out. No matter what it is, Bruce gets screwed. If we order lunch, his never comes. If we all get stationery with the show's logo and our names on it, his is either misspelled or missing. Director's chairs? His isn't there.

Bruce's first script airs. He gets a call from his mother on the East Coast, where the show airs three hours earlier.

"I thought you said you wrote the episode."

"I did."

"Then why wasn't your name on it?"

Turns out someone forgot to put any writer credits on the episode. This could only happen to Bruce.

* * *

Bruce has the office adjacent to ours. He also has as foul a mouth as Jane's. They go at each other good-naturedly to see who can outdo whom in vulgarities.

Jane barges into Bruce's pitch-black office, where he works with the blinds drawn, typing on his little laptop in the dark, calls him an asshole and runs out, slamming the door behind her. Bruce follows as fast as he can, opening the door to our office and barging in as he screams for her to "suck his cock."

Which is followed by Jane saying, "Bruce? I'd like you to meet my mother."

* * *

Jane's parents visit us on *Anything But Love* — divorced (and not happily) for years, they barely speak. As luck would have it, they both decide to visit Jane on the same day and come to a taping — separately, of course. Because all guests get seated in the same area, John and Joan Milmore find themselves sitting next to each other. If that isn't bad enough for Jane, the stand-up comedian warming up the audience arbitrarily picks them out while he's working the crowd, and forces them to not only hug, but at the urging of the audience to kiss. Backstage watching this spectacle unfold, a horrified Jane makes Bruce Rasmussen sound like a nun.

Her mother swears Jane set it up.

* * *

I'm not sure what's happening. It seems Jane and I have less to do as actors every week. Edited out into being glorified extras. Is it because it's a new show and there are plenty of more important actors to service? Or do they think we stink? Jane thinks the former. I always think the worst.

* * *

Anything But Love gives me my first opportunity to learn about editing. Peter is open to teach the process to anyone who wants to learn. He also tutors me about working with the studio and network by relaying all his discussions with them. After a read-through or a run-through, many show runners wait to hear what they did wrong from the network executive sent to cover the show, and then they have to tap-dance around their notes or fight for what they believe in.

Peter never lets them talk first. He starts each note session, with his writers present, by telling the studio and network what needs fixing, what works well, and what will work better tomorrow, and he does so with such intelligence and clarity that you'd have to be an idiot to disagree with him.

* * *

There is a common practice of show runners' approving storylines before they officially get network or studio approval. About twice a year, due to time constraints, you assume the story will be approved, assign it to a writer, and send them off "to script," then you pitch the story to the network for approval after the fact. Nine times out of 10, the story gets approved with some minor adjustment, and you fill the writer in on the change, and he or she keeps going without losing too much time.

We're writing one of the rare episodes they veto.

In the story that Peter approved without network permission, Robin is divorced. Her ex-husband (to be played by John Ritter) keeps calling to see her, and Robin, still madly in love with him, thinks it's because he wants her back. Marty and Hannah, undercover on an assignment for the magazine, discover Robin's ex-husband is gay. Now Marty and Hannah have to tell Robin before she finds out on her own.

Unfortunately, the night before Peter pitches the show that we are already writing, *Thirtysomething* airs an episode with a gay theme, which offends too many viewers and advertisers. The mandate comes down from ABC: "No gay-themed episodes." Our episode is dead.

Peter apologizes for wasting our time, and then he explains that even dumber than their decision to drop the story entirely is the fact that 20th Century Fox refuses to pay us for our work unless we actually turn in a script. So we're instructed to finish the episode anyway, knowing it will never be shot.

So we do, overnight, with vile jokes in it. Knowing no one is going to see it, and that it will never air, we write the script complete with deliberately tasteless "fisting" jokes and "butt plug" jokes and worse.

The other writers love it. Apparently so does everyone at 20th Century Fox, because some production assistant unwittingly distributes it the same way all the other scripts are distributed.

Jane and I run into the wardrobe guy for our show in a Tower Record store.

"I loved page 16!"

* * *

As the season progresses, Jane and I are getting more and more frustrated. As actors, anytime we get a laugh in rehearsal, the following day Jamie and Richard get our jokes. As writers, after meticulously working on scripts, midweek Peter invariably throws out things that are working to go off in new directions with stories that make no sense to me.

On top of it all, we stay until 3 a.m. every night. On *Newhart* we never stayed for dinner once the entire season.

* * *

One early morning after an all-nighter, I wake up to a frantic phone call from Peter to get to the studio as fast as possible. The scene we all wrote at 3 in the morning where workaholic Joe Maher's cat commits suicide out of loneliness — even writing a little cat suicide note before it hangs itself over the litter box — somehow doesn't read particularly believable in the light of day. We all race to the studio early to rewrite it before anyone reads it and we embarrass ourselves.

Nothing I've seen written as the sun comes up is ever good. So why do we keep doing it?

* * *

Jane and I love writing "Bang, You're Dead," an episode that will star Corbin Bernsen from *L.A. Law* as Marty's psychiatrist. Corbin's character meets and begins to date Hannah, which drives Marty insane (because, of course, Marty is secretly in love with Hannah). To top everything, the psychiatrist has a fatal heart attack while in bed with Hannah, prompting Marty's accusation, "You killed my shrink!"

We work on the storyline with the other writers, laughing up a storm making tasteless dead-guy-in-the-sack jokes, none of which we would ever use in the script. A woman from our show bursts into tears and runs out of the room.

"What's the matter with her?"

One of the writers informs us this woman was having sex with a guy who died of a heart attack and the storyline is too close to home. The women in the room are horrified to hear this news. Not the guys. They're impressed.

The final scene in our "dead shrink show" has Marty having a session with his dearly departed therapist in the funeral home (a corpse literally covered with Richard's lines). It's his most profound session, even though the guy's dead — and, of course, says nothing.

After Jane and I painstakingly work every nuance of the final scene, Peter decides the monologue in which Marty has an epiphany and talks about his true feelings for Hannah isn't important. Instead he should talk about death in a general sense.

The playwright in me goes crazy. We've planted seeds throughout the entire episode that need a payoff. We've made Marty act like an absolute jackass to Hannah in an early scene. Without later explaining his behavior (he's in love with her, reacting as he does out of frustration and jealousy), Marty is simply a nasty asshole with no justification. But *with* that awakening, it's the best script we've written.

Peter doesn't care. "Some people write A to B to C. I like A to B to Q."

I tell Jane, "Peter doesn't know what he's talking about."

"What can we do about it?"

My youthful arrogance and ego make the decision a simple one. "There's only one thing to do. Get in the car, Jane. We're quitting."

* * *

We meet with Peter, who is completely confused and utterly unaware there were any problems before this moment. We stand our ground. Peter is gracious enough to let us out of our contract. We agree that Jane and I will finish out the last two episodes of the initial order of 13 and will write two more scripts after we're gone.

The studio executives go crazy. Vice presidents are standing in my parking space at the studio waiting for me when I arrive for work the next day. They corner me as I step out of the car to try and talk me out of leaving.

Agents call our houses at all hours of the night to talk us into staying with the show — and dumping our agent who must be an idiot to let us leave such a hot property — our private numbers given to them by the studio executives.

The fact is, I don't know how to write Peter's way. And I put too much into the scripts to sit by and watch them gutted and rewritten an hour before we shoot them. When the execs can't get through to me, they call Jane to talk her into breaking up the writing team so she can stay on without me. We actually hear the cliché, "You'll never work in this town again," from a bigshot at 20th who wears a bad hairpiece.

Adding salt to the wound, he yells at Peter for letting us act on the show in the first place when the roles should have gone to "real" actors. (Did I mention it was a *laughably* bad hairpiece?)

Peter stands his ground. "If they're not happy here, let them go."

* * *

Peter's a class act. Despite all he's done for us, we leave his show, yet he's cool about it. He even gives my character a fun sendoff. It's decided that my on-screen character Harold will get fired in my last episode after he makes yet another stupid suggestion for a magazine article.

In an eye-opening moment, this week's director Michael Lessac pulls me aside to say, "You're not in the theater playing to the back of the balcony, Billy. Do less." Oh, why wasn't he here 13 episodes ago?

The final moment I film as Harold has me flailing behind Catherine's office window with a live boa constrictor around my neck, after it's revealed a pet shop in the building was broken into and all the animals are missing. As the "snake wrangler" places the 30-foot snake around my neck, I ask how he trains these things.

His answer: "We can't. They have brains the size of a pea."

I ask: "Well, then what keeps him from tightening around my neck and killing me?"

There is a long beat as he thinks about it, and then he answers: "Nothing."

I do it anyway.

* * *

One month after Jane and I leave the show, we go into development at Grant-Tribune Entertainment to create and sell our own TV shows. We also break up as a couple for good. But we are offered such a ridiculous amount of money to develop original programming we decide to suck it up and stay together as a writing team, working through the breakup, the fights, the broken hearts, and watching each other date other people — all without ever missing one single day of work.

How? We learn to compartmentalize. We become writing partners only, and anything else is shoved into a box. We don't speak after the workday ends. During the day we're professionally polite, but we do attack each other's work a little more than we used to. We'll make it work. So what if I'm emotionally numb for a few years. All our energy will go into our shows.

We use the anger/heartbreak/insanity to write the remaining *Anything But Love* script we owe Peter. It turns out to be our best script.

In the story, Richard's character breaks up with his girlfriend right as they walk into a surprise party. Everyone at the party — including the girl's parents — has overheard the humiliating breakup and proceeds to brutalize Marty in a cruel *This is Your Life* roast gone sour. We got a lot of good material out of breaking up.

As we sit in the bleachers on shoot night and hear the audience howling with laughter, I realize how much I've grown as a writer thanks to this show. I no longer write gag to gag. Peter has taught me to keep things in my writing real and believable. That a laugh isn't the most important thing in a scene. That paring down the show to its emotional core makes everything stronger. That writing linear isn't the only way to tell a story. Why didn't I realize any of this when I worked here? I thought I knew it all. But I didn't. Peter Noah was right.

The best moments of *Anything But Love* are the small ones between Jamie and Richard. My favorite scenes are when they sit around talking, long after each episode ends in the traditional sense. No big climax, just a small emotional ending. Great stuff.

I watch the show. I laugh my brains out. And I wonder what on earth I was thinking. We were series regulars on a Top Ten show and part of the best writing staff in the business. And we quit.

What a great show.

What an idiot.

Actor. Asshole. Same thing.

WORKING THE WEEKEND

Consulting on "Sydney"

Development deals are peculiar. The studio pays us a ridiculous amount of money, giving us an office and an assistant, to create and sell new shows. We work on our own timeline, and when we're ready to reveal our finished product, we pitch it to the studio. Then, with their approval, they set up network pitch sessions and we try to hit a bull's-eye.

In between sales pitches and creating shows, we consult on other people's shows a few days a week. I hear that some people working in development also play golf, take extended vacations, and write plays.

The first show we consult on is *Sydney*, starring *One Day at a Time* star Valerie Bertinelli.

Writer Michael Wilson is good. He not only has created the show — which stars Valerie as a private eye who solves crimes every week — he has hired no one at all to be on the writing staff. He *is* the writing staff. He writes every single episode himself over the weekend. On Mondays, he shows up and hands scripts to the actors, the studio, and the network people — who see it for the first time — and then he starts rehearsing.

The network and the studio can't give Michael any notes, because he simply hasn't given them any material to take notes on. They don't even know the storylines before they hear the scripts read aloud. Co-stars Matthew Perry and Craig Bierko help Michael rewrite scenes

50

onstage as they rehearse them. The network is powerless to stop this because, as the CBS exec tells me, "We have no shows to replace this with."

Jane and I visit the show once or twice a week to help Michael out, give a few notes, write a few jokes, and then go home. They call it "consulting." To us, it's helping out people while we don't have anything else going on. We don't take any credit on the show despite Valerie and Michael asking us to take one every week. It feels completely unnecessary. If a joke we write gets a laugh, that's enough. People are credit-crazy out here.

Valerie is as sweet as I thought she'd be. No star ego. She's a real pro with a sunny personality that's positive and fun to be around, creating a warm family feeling on the set. And she's game to try anything. I really like her.

Matthew Perry plays Valerie's younger brother, who's a cop, and he keeps giving himself incredibly physical entrances — popping through the door at running speeds, tripping and flipping over couches, or crashing into bookcases. The guy will be on a walker in a few years. He doesn't know how to take a fall at all. He smashes himself into things. It's a wonder he doesn't knock himself unconscious.

Matthew has an odd delivery, very dry, great with sarcasm. He's stealing scenes left and right. A little too selfishly for my taste, but there's no denying he's funny.

Craig Bierko, who plays Valerie's love interest, is a joy to write for. Craig is absolutely the best physical comedian I've seen since Dick Van Dyke. As it turns out he's a huge fan of Mr. Van Dyke and has studied him in detail.

Barney Martin, who starred on Broadway as "Mr. Cellophane" in the Bob Fosse musical *Chicago* and played Liza Minnelli's father in *Arthur*, plays the bartender father figure for Valerie. We hit it off instantly.

I notice the network has it out for Barney.

"He can't learn his lines."

"He can't learn his lines."

"We should fire him. He can't learn his lines."

In response, Jane and I write Barney a full-page monologue during a rewrite. The next day, he nails every syllable. We never hear the note again.

Danny Baldwin plays a neighborhood barfly, doing an exact impression of comic Rodney Dangerfield. Every line he delivers makes me laugh.

Valerie could not have stronger co-stars.

* * *

This is the first time I've seen a star sit in on the network notes. After every run-through, the network gives notes to Michael, Jane, Valerie, and me. Then after Valerie leaves the room, Michael calls the network to see if they have any additional notes they couldn't offer in front of Valerie about her performance. Then after the network hangs up, Jane and I give additional notes *we* couldn't offer in front of Valerie (e.g., "Change her costume in that scene").

* * *

In addition to punching up jokes, Jane plays the recurring role of Craig's fiancée from hell. She's hilarious. I marry Valerie and Craig in the final episode as "Father Van Zandt," having a great time cracking the cast up with my sanctimonious minister voice. We have an absolute ball on this show.

* * *

Michael has written 20 of the first 20 scripts, in addition to doing all the other executive producer duties of running a show. We've offered to give him a break and write one — with notice — but Michael wants to do it all himself. I can't blame him. He's getting away with something I've never heard of. No writing staff and no network notes. And it's as good as anything else on the air.

Jane hears a rumor that we're going to be asked to write the final script over the weekend. I say, "There is no way in hell I'm writing a script in two days. We've offered all season long. Forget it. There's nothing Michael can say that will get me to write a script."

Our intercom buzzes.

"Billy, it's Michael."

"Hi, Michael. What's up?"

"Could you do me a huge favor? My sister — you've seen her at the tapings, in the wheelchair? Well, she has diabetes. They've already cut off her legs. And this weekend they're cutting off her arms. Could you write the script for Monday?"

It was on his desk in 18 hours.

& JANE MILMORE

Who Writes What

Who writes what? People constantly ask whether I wrote this or Jane wrote that. The answer is pretty simple. If you liked it, I wrote it. If it wasn't funny, then Jane wrote it.

OK, none of that is true, but this is as good a place as any to explain how we work.

There is no formula for writing a script with a partner — or writing a script at all. Every script is different. Some are outlined. Some take on a life of their own. Mostly Jane and I talk out a general story, and then I write the rough first draft. Then Jane edits and rewrites my first draft. Then I put back all the funny things I wrote that she didn't like. Then we fight. Then most of what I put back comes out again.

Finally content with a "writers' first draft" — which means no one besides the two of us reads it yet — we go through each scene together. Out loud. And we edit and tweak as we go. We mark up what needs to be better and then pitch on those spots and rewrite. Then I take another pass on my own. Then Jane takes another pass. Then I put back things I liked that she cut out. And finally, content with what we have, we go through the script as each character to make sure each role tracks.

And then I squeeze back in something Jane still doesn't realize is funny.

Then we let it sit. Then we come back to it with fresh eyes. Then we edit and rewrite again. Two or three times of this. And that's when we let a few close friends see our script.

Then we do a joke pass to make sure we're still laughing at everything.

And that officially becomes our "first draft."

From that point on, the rehearsal process with the director and the actors — and the audience — dictates the rest.

Jane is quicker than I am with jokes. I craft mine carefully. But with Jane, whatever comes off the top of her head is usually brilliant and perfect for the moment. If I ask her to repeat what she just said she has no idea and will cobble together a less funny version of what she originally said. So I'm quick to write down the first thing out of her mouth.

The only consistent thing in all our scripts is that I hog the computer because (1) Jane can't spell and (2) this way I get the last word.

* * *

The bad part of being a team? Whereas every writer has his or her own strength and weakness, the other member of the team must pick up the slack. For instance, I don't like writing the sentimental parts of a script, so Jane does that. As a result, I never developed those muscles. The other bad part: We make the same amount of money on each script as single writers. So we each make half of what every other writer we work with gets paid.

The good part of being a team? There's always somebody to watch your back, support you when you doubt yourself, laugh at your jokes, and keep you from writing insulting emails to someone who might deserve it. And, of course, there's always somebody to blame when someone's jokes don't work (Jane's, after she *reworks* them).

NOBODY WINS AN EMMY

The I Love Lucy pilot and The Emmy Awards

"I found the *Lucy* pilot!"

Bud Grant, former president of CBS and current president of the studio we're under contract to, has located the *I Love Lucy* pilot — 10 months after Lucy's death.

The pilot footage has been missing and unseen for 40 years. I didn't know it still existed.

In 1950, Lucille Ball and Desi Arnaz produced their own television pilot for the amazingly low sum of $5,000. They made two copies. One for CBS, and a second copy for a clown named Pepito who guest-starred in the show. Not only was Pepito a world-famous vaudeville clown, he put together the comedy cello act that Lucy and Desi toured with a year earlier to prove to CBS that this interracial couple who were married in real life (Lucy "the good ol' American girl" and Desi "the Cuban") were acceptable to audiences as an actual couple.

Forty years later, CBS has lost its copy. And the widow of Pepito the clown has no idea what she has in her possession.

As a child, Bud Grant's girlfriend was a dance student of Pepito's wife and has kept in touch throughout the years. On one occasion when she's visiting with Bud, they sit in the living room as Pepito's widow shows home movies and are surprised when they see a rare piece of television history sandwiched between birthday footage and family Christmas movies.

The next day, Bud races next door to our office — where the autographed photo of Lucy hangs on the wall behind my desk — and asks if Jane and I want to produce a television special to unveil the missing Lucy pilot. Jane says, "You don't even have to ask Billy. And I have no choice."

* * *

It's fascinating to watch the film. Lucille Ball hasn't yet found her Lucy character. The sets are cheap, and the walls shake. The pilot shows off Desi Arnaz and his band more than Lucy. No Ethel or Fred.

Still, the essence of the show is there. Lucy wants to get into Ricky's act. Ricky wants Lucy to stay home. And their love for each other shines through loud and clear.

We go to CBS to sell this 34-minute piece of TV history and are promptly told the network already owns the rights. We say: "You may own the rights, but we have the footage. If you want to see it again, we need a deal in place for a television special, plus a big, fat check for Pepito's widow."

CBS agrees, telling us it plans to take the original footage and edit it down to a half hour. Sacrilege.

We refuse. "Give us an hour of airtime, and we'll fill in around the episode with the story of the show's creation — or forget the whole thing."

We get our full-hour special. And Pepito's widow gets a nice, big, fat check.

* * *

Before we can celebrate, CBS informs us we have to turn in the completed special in under three weeks to make "sweeps week." Otherwise CBS will edit the footage, as originally intended. They assume we'll never make the deadline. They don't realize who they're dealing with. Years of watching episodes twice a day, along with all the interviews ever given, and all the *Lucy* specials ever produced, make this a piece of cake for me. I'm able to tell the show's researchers exactly what Lucy said in which interview and when it aired and where to get it. We can have the story of the series' creation told in Lucy's and Desi's own words.

We hire our friend Tom Watson, Lucy's longtime assistant, as a researcher. He's invaluable in helping us track down what we need.

Barbara Walters sends us the interview footage with Lucy from *Good Morning, America* that I asked for — a rare thing at the time for an ABC show to help out a CBS show. I also order new pristine prints of almost every *Lucy* episode struck so I can pull film clips and put my favorite moments together for a final *I Love Lucy* montage over Desi Arnaz singing the title song (from the *Lucy* birthday episode).

Director David Steinberg films my old bosses, *Lucy* writers Bob Carroll Jr. and Madelyn Davis, who reminisce about the making of the pilot. The late Jess Oppenheimer's son Greg helps us pay tribute to his father, the show's creator and executive producer, by sending us pilot photos from behind the scenes that no one has ever seen.

We do it all in less than three weeks. Never enters my mind for a second that we couldn't. I'm grinning ear to ear the entire time.

The only trouble we have is getting someone to host the evening. I want Lucie Arnaz but, without even reading our script, she declines. Her mother hasn't been gone even a year, so I understand and don't pursue it. We start to go after Carol Burnett, when the phone rings.

It's Lucie Arnaz.

In order to get the rights to show footage of her parents on our special, "Little Lucie" — now in charge of their estates — must read and approve the script. Once she does, she realizes we're paying tribute to her father even more so than her mother, and she gladly says she'll come aboard and host the show.

"If you ask anybody else, I'll picket the studio!"

Lucie rightfully claims no one in Hollywood remembers her father properly and that she's grateful someone is finally paying him his due. She says, "Nowhere in Hollywood, except the Latin community, is my father's contribution to the business even acknowledged. Not one studio building bears his name. Not one street. No television history books ever mention him, except as my mother's straight man."

I'm happy to oblige. Desi Arnaz invented the sitcom as we know it today. He created the three-camera technique that every live show still uses. He started the live studio audience. He shot *Lucy* on film instead of tape, resulting in most lucrative cash cow in the entertainment industry — the rerun.

Along the way, Desilu Productions was responsible for *I Love Lucy, Mission: Impossible, Our Miss Brooks, The Untouchables, The Ann Sothern Show, December Bride, Mannix,* and *Wyatt Earp,* among many, many others. (And ultimately, once Lucy took over the studio from Desi, a little show called *Star Trek.*)

* * *

For *I Love Lucy:* The Very First Show, we recreate the *I Love Lucy* set to scale, and Lucie does the wrap-around narration. No one realizes it until Lucie walks in, but the day she works is the first anniversary of her mother's death. She never falters and is very professional. I hope we are doing her parents proud.

Our next battle with the network is when we decide to give the CBS publicity department absolutely *nothing* to show as a commercial. No more than five seconds of film. Right up until one half-hour before we air the show when we deliver the finished special.

We aren't being difficult for the sake of being difficult. The lost pilot has similarities to an episode Lucy and Desi did after the show had been sold — where Lucy tries to get into Ricky's night club act by doing her performing seal bit. This act had been part of the vaudeville routine Pepito had created for them, and they worked it into the pilot.

I'm afraid that if people see even a second of that footage, they'll think they've seen this episode before and not bother to watch our special at all.

We give CBS nothing. With no choice, the network's PR people are forced to be creative. They not only do a fantastic job of whetting people's appetites, they drive the country crazy to find out what is on that film.

* * *

Everybody watches it. We are the highest-rated show of the *season*. *The Big Bang Theory* at its height got a 6.2 rating and a 20 share. We got a 21.7 rating and a 38 share. That's the percentage of televisions turned on watching you at the same time. Impressive. Everybody still loves Lucy.

* * *

Emmy night. Nominated for "Best Informational Special."

Could we win?

We had no idea, but I did clear a space on my mantel before I left for the event. The truth is, I'd already received my award — seeing the famous *I Love Lucy* heart close over footage of Lucy and Desi with the words "Produced by Billy Van Zandt & Jane Milmore" right in the center. It doesn't get any better than that.

My date and I pull up in our car. The door opens. A horde of photographers leans in. One guy peers over his camera, then turns to the others and says, "It's nobody." They move on.

* * *

Inside we sit at a table between The Simpsons writers and the *Tracy Ullman Show* writers. As the night goes by, we watch the Simpson/Ullman tables get covered with award after award.

Then it's our turn.

"And the Emmy goes to…"

It's a tie. The first winner is an *American Masters* tribute to Bob Fosse. It seems like it takes these people three days to walk up there and give their speeches. I think back to my childhood: watching episode after episode of *Lucy*; studying the masters — of both comic acting and comic writing; knowing what I wanted to do with my life from the age of 10 because of Lucy, Ricky, Fred, and Ethel, and Bob, Madelyn, and Jess; finally the thrill of meeting and working with Lucy — all culminating in this one final tribute. It's too perfect.

Besides, who isn't going to vote for Lucy?

Apparently, the people on the voting committee.

* * *

I don't recall the second winner of the category. All I remember is it wasn't us. And discovering there's a reason they close the bar during the awards ceremony.

I still swear they must have counted the votes wrong. And to this day, Jane still keeps telling me, "Let it go!"

I never will.

PARIS OR NEW JERSEY?

How I spent my summer vacation

The problem with selling something to TV at the last minute on the West Coast while plotting to do a play on the East Coast at the same time is that, well, you don't have time to write the play for the East Coast.

All the time we were selling, writing, and producing the *Lucy* special, here's what went on behind the scenes on the East Coast:

Our usual theater, back home in New Jersey, needs to advertise our latest show for our annual trip home, where we debut an original play every spring, a decades-long tradition. Most TV writers go to Paris or Hawaii when the television seasons end. Jane and I go to New Jersey and do original plays with our gang of incredibly funny actor friends called The Unofficial Van Zandt/Milmore Repertory Company — the same actors we've been working with since the early Dam Site days.

It's a great, fun time, and it restores my sanity for the rest of the year to get me through the TV grind, and through the years Jane and I get to put a lot of the local theater kids who work on our crew through college by offering an annual scholarship.

Usually, the way it works is Jane and I settle on a play to write by January at the latest, and we call actors we want to cast in February telling them to hold the dates for the show in May and June. Then we write the play. Yes, it's too short a time, which is why we rewrite them daily during the runs and again before we publish them with Samuel French after the runs close.

That's how it *usually* works.

Not this time.

It's January, and the theater needs a title for the upcoming May-June run. Knowing we'll have plenty of time to write it, we call it *Do Not Disturb*, figuring whatever it turns out to be can take place in a hotel room. Then we go about trying to sell our TV pilots to the networks.

In February, the theater back home advertises *Do Not Disturb*, and we start selling out the run.

Not having sold a TV show this season, we finally sit down to put pen to paper (or rather, fingers to keyboard), with plenty of time to write the play, and that's when the *I Love Lucy* pilot falls into our laps. The second half of February and the month of March are all about selling the special to CBS and writing the script.

In mid-March, we get a frantic call from our set designer back East. "When do I get a script?" I say, "You don't. Build me a hotel room with a door over here, a closet over there, an exit to a bathroom here, a picture window there, and a big bed dead center. Think The Plaza in New York."

We can figure out the show later. Back to our special.

They start building our set 3,000 miles away — for a sold-out show that isn't written yet.

The TV special shoots in April, as the theater actors from back East start calling.

"When do we get a script?"

"Not yet."

"What am I playing?"

"You'll see. You'll love it!"

We don't have one word written. We open in four weeks.

Luckily *I Love Lucy: The Very First Show* goes easily enough for Jane and me to finally spend time in our offices putting together the play. Edward Albee wrote some of his plays in three weeks' time; we can do this in the four we have left.

We discover we aren't Edward Albee. We can't come up with a thing. We decide to write a series of vignettes that all take place in this one hotel room, thinking it would easier. It's not. Instead of one play, we now have to write six plays.

One week before rehearsals begin, we have one vignette finished. One, based entirely on a trip I took with a girlfriend up to Solvang, the touristy kitschy Swedish capital of California where I saw these insanely funny big-horned Valkyrie hats, bought three, and told Jane I didn't care what our next play was but it had to have three big-horned Valkyrie hats in it.

Jane and I show up for the first rehearsal in New Jersey with a cast of actors that has no idea what they're playing or what the show is about, with nothing in our hands but one vignette and three Viking helmets. We get calls from journalists who want to interview us about a play that they don't realize isn't written.

Rather than admit we have nothing, the first day of rehearsal I announce to our actors that we're rehearsing a new way this year: one vignette at a time. And once this first sketch is rehearsed perfectly, we'll move on to the second, and so on, until we put it all together. That gives us two days to write each vignette until we open.

We rehearse the only one we have — a crazy sketch about a bellhop who is blackmailed by pranksters who are pretending to film a Viking porno movie. (See how I got the helmets into the show?)

That night we go back to Jane's house and say, "OK, what's the second scene about?" And we spend the night writing a new vignette about a couple with wedding jitters.

We pull this off, one vignette after another, until we get to the dress rehearsal when we put the whole show together. And that's when we realize the show is too short. We need one more vignette. The actors are on to us at this point but going along, equal parts amused and horrified. I say, "OK, I'll write one more scene, but I'm not learning any more lines." We create a scene where Jane is on a date with a new guy and stalked by her ex. I play the ex. And he's mute.

The show opens. The reviews are great. And singled out? The scene we wrote the night before we opened and the symbolism of the ex-boyfriend who has no voice.

Writing fast for TV saved us. Sometimes when you don't have time to think and second-guess yourself, the craft itself can get you through — as can three Viking helmets.

But if we ever call you and ask you to be in one of our plays, it's probably smart to ask to see the script before you say yes.

"GET IN THE CAR, JANE!"

Witt-Thomas, Dorothy Lamour, and "Nurses"

We land our first jobs as "Supervising Producers." On one of the studio lots that Lucy and Desi used to own. Plus time off midseason to produce and star in our first play in Los Angeles.

It can't get any better than this.

Paul Witt and Tony Thomas made their mark producing *Soap, Benson, The Practice, Empty Nest,* and their best-known show, *The Golden Girls.*

Nurses — with the pilot written by Susan Harris — was supposed to be an *Empty Nest* spinoff starring Park Overall, who played Richard Mulligan's smartass nurse on that series. Somewhere between writing the pilot and putting it on the air, Park somehow isn't involved anymore, and the show now stars comedienne Stephanie Hodge, whose stand-up act's highlight is her talking dirty in fast speed.

We arrive at the studio to discover that *Nurses* has changed from the big, slapstick "*Night Court* in a hospital" show we signed on to do into a caring, loving hospital show with "good nursing moments." No gags. No broad jokes. No slapstick.

We're shown to our office, and as we set down our things, I ask where our assistant is supposed to sit.

"What assistant?"

"Our assistant."

"What are you talking about? You don't get an assistant." "

Sure we do. It's in our contract."

"No, it isn't."

"Yes, it is. We've talked Jane's sister Maureen into quitting a great job in New York and flying out here to work for us. She's literally in the air right now."

"That's not the studio's problem."

Despite a deal memo that they deny ever writing, we're told they won't pay our assistant a salary, nor give her an office to answer the phone. She can sit on the extra chair in our little office and answer phones around us as we write scripts if we like, and we can feel free to pay her out of our own salary, as well as buy her a health plan on our own dime.

We're not off to a good start.

* * *

The man from Witt-Thomas who originally okayed our deal memo comes around to see how happy all "his writers" are. Catching him completely off-guard, Jane chews his head off. By the time she finishes with him, he leaves our office in tears, literally sobbing loudly into his hands.

This is going to be a long season.

* * *

Instead of having the writing staff come up with original stories, we're told to take plot lines from *The Practice*, a Danny Thomas doctor vehicle — from the 1970s.

We're supposed to write the one-line storylines on color-coordinated index cards, which Paul and Tony will mix and match, putting each Blue card A-Story (the main storyline) with an unconnected Yellow card B-Story (the smaller storyline).

It's an assembly line.

* * *

We arrive at the first run-through to see only two chairs set up. One is for Paul, and one is for Tony. We stand behind them like steerage.

* * *

It's shoot night of the first episode. Unlike *Newhart*, where we sat in the audience to laugh along with the crowd, or *Anything But Love*, where we stood behind the cameras ready to rewrite jokes, the writers on *Nurses* sit in the little control booth — silently — behind Paul and Tony, who talk and joke to one other as if no one else is in the room. We're instructed not to even whisper unless addressed directly.

I ask, "Then why are we even here?"

"Because they're paying you to be here. Shh."

"But we're not doing anything."

"Shhhh."

* * *

NBC President Brandon Tartikoff calls for Paul. Paul smiles at us and then purposefully puts him on hold and makes him wait for a full minute before picking up the call.

* * *

When he's not putting people on hold, Paul pontificates from his vast knowledge of, well, everything. He's incredibly well read, and it's irritating.

We decide to bone up on something to outdo him. We choose The Punic Wars. Casually one night at a taping I let slip that I'd read some-one was writing a new Broadway musical based on Hannibal and his elephants.

Jane says, "I read the same article. It's a show called *O Hannibal*." And that is everyone's cue. Suddenly, we writers are off discussing — in depth — trivia about Hannibal's trek through the mountains.

"Amazing isn't it? 100,000 men on elephants."

"Hey. Was it the first or second Punic War?"

"Second. 218 B.C. His father commanded the first Punic War."

"Oh, that's right. Hamilcar Barca, wasn't it?"

"Yes. Hamilcar Barca. Hannibal and the elephants were the second Punic War."

Suddenly Paul Witt jumps in: "Yet thanks to the Battle of Zama, they still they weren't able to conquer Rome."

* * *

Nurses starts out with a writing staff of about 10, and every Friday someone gets fired — never to be replaced. Every Monday the writers come to work and scramble to see which new bigger office is empty and available. The running joke is not to answer your phone on the weekend, because everyone gets fired over the phone on Saturday mornings.

Even with the empty offices, the studio still refuses to give our assistant an office to answer our phones.

* * *

An executive producer's job is to make every creative decision regarding scripts, cast, directors, designs, publicity, music, props, sound, music, editing, and scheduling, and do all of this while sticking to the budget and pleasing the network, the studio, and, ultimately, the audience. On top of all that, you have to find the time, energy, and talent to write a few episodes yourself. That's what a show runner does.

Ours doesn't even seem able to pick a restaurant to order lunch from.

* * *

We stay all night. Every night. And Saturdays. We order in three meals a day while we sit there forbidden to talk, waiting for an explanation of what to fix in each script.

Most days we spend eight hours of every day just staring at the wall — or, in the case of one writer, just drawing pictures all day long in a notebook.

The only break in the torture is when we hear: "Don't make plans for the weekend. I'm sure we'll be working."

The pressure is so intense that we all threaten to kill writer Eric Gilliland if he orders another hot turkey sandwich for the 10th day in a row.

* * *

Since I'm not accomplishing anything in the writer's room, I ask Paul and Tony if I might sit in on an editing session.

I watch a rough cut of one episode. Paul asks what notes I have. He and Tony stare at me with their arms folded, daring me to give a note. I give a rather simple note of holding a reaction shot, as opposed to the quick cut that's in the edit we just viewed.

Paul rolls his eyes and says: "Oh, thank you, Billy, we never would have thought of that!"

Tony: "You can go now."

I guess they don't need any help with the editing.

* * *

Chris Thompson (*Bosom Buddies*) is "here to save the show," Paul announces in front of the writers when he introduces him to the cast — who aren't aware the show needs saving.

There are three chairs at the run-through that day. One for Paul. One for Tony. And one for Chris. I sit in that one.

After the run-through, we go back to the room to fix the script, and Chris starts dictating. Our executive producer, who had one time been a production assistant, takes the legal pad from our writer's assistant and starts scribbling Chris's notes word for word. The rest of us leave the room. Neither Chris nor our boss notices.

The next day the actors rehearse Chris's script. None of it works. Chris suddenly doesn't work here anymore.

* * *

On Labor Day as we stare at more walls; we're told, "Don't make any plans for Christmas, because you'll all be working."

* * *

Paul's wife, writer Susan Harris, comes to the set to see a run-through of the one episode she's decided to write for the show. Escorted by Paul, and looking like Norma Desmond with big sunglasses, she enters the soundstage. She doesn't say hello to anyone nor make eye contact. We're instructed not to speak to her unless addressed directly. Ms. Harris glides to her seat (one of three today), sits through the run-through, nods her approval to the actors, and goes home with never a word spoken.

We change nothing at all in the script. Miraculously the episode is our best — I guess when actors have time to rehearse with the same material, they can make a script better than when they just memorize new pages handed to them at the last minute.

* * *

Eric Gilliland is fired. Not because of the turkey sandwiches, but because he has done a rewrite on another turkey — a script that just stank to begin with. And a basic rule of thumb on a sitcom is once a script has a certain smell to it, you can never get it out. Plus, Eric made the mistake of answering his phone on a Saturday.

Eric had attempted a rewrite, but the jokes he added were so mean-spirited he was let go. It's a script about an older woman falling in love with a younger man, and most of the unflattering "older woman" jokes might as well have our producer's name stamped on them.

Since Eric is contractually guaranteed money for all episodes produced this year, for the rest of the season he calls us every single day to laugh at us from home where he makes the same amount of money watering his lawn as we do working like oxen 20 hours a day.

* * *

When the studio realizes that part of our contract allows us to leave at 6 p.m. on Fridays to perform in the West Coast premiere of our play *Drop Dead!* they go ballistic. Again, the man who reneged on our deal memo is called on the carpet and reamed out for agreeing to this. Pathetically, he has just recovered from the measles, and as they yell at him we can't help but notice with his pockmarked face, his big red bow tie, and the water pouring from his eyes, he resembles a clown from a Stephen King novel.

Our play is crazy-successful and stars Jonathan D. Mack, Glenn Kelman, Jane, and me from the New York cast, along with Rose Marie from *The Dick Van Dyke Show*, Barney Martin from *Seinfeld*, Donny Most from *Happy Days,* and the woman who will eventually become my wife and the mother of my kids, Adrienne Barbeau.

Drop Dead! not only gets us through *Nurses*, it brings us friends for life. And spouses: I get Adrienne. Jane marries one of our producers. To show you how far we've come as friends at this point and how little we see each other as anything other than friends, one day Jane innocently tells me how hard it is being with her Richard Gere lookalike boyfriend. "It's weird how much attention he gets. I never dated a good-looking guy before."

No offense taken.

The play is fun to do — too much so at times. I direct it, but frankly after opening night, it just turns into a comedic free-for-all. Each sight gag in the show turns into three, and we all do our best to try and top one another and crack each other up.

We even have a private contest during one performance called "Jerry Lewis Night," where you have to work in a Jerry Lewis impression somewhere in the show. Craig Bierko wins that one. But seeing Rose Marie do a "Hey, Lady" is pretty great.

Another great thrill is watching Bob Carroll Jr. and Madelyn Davis in the audience laughing their heads off. There's always that *Lucy* connection.

The best part of the play is, of course, meeting Adrienne. I had originally offered the role of Mona the TV star to Tina Louise from *Gilligan's Island*, whose agent turned us down. When Adrienne and I marry a year and a half later, a friend sends a card that said, "Good thing you didn't cast Tina Louise."

No one from Witt-Thomas ever comes to the show, and throughout our sold-out run no one mentions the rave reviews from every single paper in town. They pretend it isn't happening. The only one who comes from the studio is Betty White, and she's not even on our show.

* * *

After six episodes and a weekly firing of perfectly good writers, the writing staff consists of just Jane, Bruce Ferber, and me. We're allowed to go home only when it looks like rain, because our boss doesn't want her dog to get wet.

* * *

Jane, who is not always the quickest to pick up on such things, innocently mentions one day, "I'm starting to get the feeling she doesn't like me."

Bruce and I both answer at the same time. "Doesn't like you? She hates you!" and we laugh harder than we have since we started the job.

* * *

After three months, no new stories are approved. No scripts are being written. We just work 20-hour days in an office so close to the street that even with the windows shut you taste car fumes all day.

After yet another 15-minute silence one night around 4 a.m., Bruce Ferber asks what I am thinking. I say, "I'm hoping a car will crash through this window and kill me." There is a pause, and then Bruce says, "I'll go get my car if you promise me I'll die too."

We laugh so hard we can't stop. We're yelled at like we're third graders. "Stop laughing! Fine. If you're going to laugh, go home."

We bolt — and spend another hour in the parking lot laughing our heads off.

* * *

Jane and I have written a script to guest-star two elderly people falling in love. One of the two will play the grandfather of series regular comic Jeff Altman. In the episode, the grandfather not only falls in love with a woman he meets at the hospital, but he dies in the hospital bed having sex with her.

Since the audience for our show is somewhere between 50 and their own funeral, I suggest we use old Hollywood stars in the guest-star roles. The audience will love to see them all again. Paul and Tony seem to like the idea. I suggest we cast Dorothy Lamour as the old lady. I had just seen her in a production of *Follies* in Long Beach. Compared with doing a Stephen Sondheim musical, a little three-scene guest-spot on a half-hour TV show is a walk in the park.

The next thing I know it's announced Dorothy Lamour is coming in to audition.

I'm shocked. "You're making her audition?"

Paul Witt's answer: "That's the way it's done in this business. If she wants the role, she'll just have to read for it."

Paul tells us that Miss Lamour said she'd never auditioned for anything in her life — not even her Paramount movie contract. But if they wanted her that badly, she'd be more than happy to come read for them.

The next day, a gold Rolls-Royce pulls into the lot, and into our lousy little studio offices comes one of early Hollywood's all-time biggest stars — Dorothy Lamour. Right into … a waiting room with 20 other women reading for the same role!

If Miss Lamour is as incensed as I am, she doesn't show it. She is very classy and gracious about it as she radiates into the room to meet everyone and read. She is lovely. She is sweet. And she is nervous. I get very excited, looking forward to hearing all the old Bob Hope-Bing Crosby stories on the set the upcoming week.

Before the door even closes behind her, Paul announces: "Nah. Bring the next one in."

"What do you mean, 'Nah'? What's wrong with her?"

Tony agrees with his partner: "She was a little slow."

"Slow? She never auditioned before!"

Paul: "We can do better."

Subject is closed.

"What will you say to her?" I ask.

Paul looks at me as if I'm nuts. "I'm not calling her. I don't call every actor that doesn't get a role."

* * *

The next script up is the one that has been rewritten four times by four separate writers, each of whom has gotten fired after turning in their draft. It is suddenly Jane's and my turn to rewrite it, despite the fact there is nothing wrong with drafts Nos. 1–4. We write a pretty funny script, but it's decided we didn't capture it exactly right either.

We don't get the pleasure of being fired. Instead we are forced to sit in the conference room with literally nothing to do except watch homeless people on the street outside the studio check their teeth out in our street-side window while our boss sits in her office down the hall writing this gem by herself.

The next day we go to the read-through with the new script and hear the actors read. The script dies a miserable death. Immediately after the reading, in front of all the actors, the three remaining writers hear directed at us: "Well! *You* all sure have a lot of work to do!"

I walk out of the soundstage and immediately toss my script into a nearby dumpster.

"Get in the car, Jane!"

"Again?"

"Yes!"

We walk. Three months later than we should have.

Jane and I drive off the lot, never to return. My last view of Witt-Thomas is writer Bruce Ferber staring at me in my rear-view mirror as we drive away with a look of panic on his face that screams, "Noooo!"

* * *

The downside of quitting is they stop paying us. And since every other show in town is already staffed up, we're out of commission for the rest of the season.

We work out of my apartment — with Maureen staked out in a spare bedroom wondering what the hell she's gotten into — as we write more plays, and occasionally help Eric Gilliland water his lawn.

* * *

The upside of quitting is I get my sanity back. Away from the assembly line I find my way back to the craft and joy of writing comedy.

Jane's sister moves up from my guest bedroom office to become a successful television producer (*Martin*, *The Tom Show*) and eventually VP of Production for the CW television network.

Nurses stayed on the air for three years. I never watched a single episode.

My time there taught me how not to run a show. In addition to being psychotically organized and appreciative of people who work for me, in all the years since, I've never made established stars audition, I've never kept a writer in the room for lunch, never made a staff work a Saturday, and always made sure there were enough chairs on the set.

Oh. And I learned that Hannibal lost the Battle of Zama.

BLACK — LIKE ME?

"Martin"

"How would you like to co-executive-produce a show for Martin Lawrence?"

"The chain of art galleries located in Southern California shopping malls?"

"No, the comedian."

"Never heard of him."

* * *

Writer/Producer John Bowman sends us a tape of the funniest comedian I've ever seen. The host of Russell Simmons' *Def Jam*, Martin reminds me of — and I mean this as a compliment — Jerry Lewis.

I find myself laughing at not only whatever physical bit Martin does, but at the audacity of how long he does it. Even after the laugh has long ended and most comedians move on, Martin (Lawrence) & (Jerry) Lewis keep going — mugging and milking the same gag over and over until I'd find myself laughing again at the pure gall. That takes great timing and great guts.

We say yes as soon as the tape ends.

* * *

Jane and I take the *Martin* job with two stipulations. The one from John Bowman is that we won't quit. After *Anything But Love* and *Nurses*, we have a reputation. The stipulation from us is that we'll write the male/female dynamics but will not write "black" jargon. Jane and I aren't black, and we're not going to pretend we are when we write the show. The all-black writing staff can change our dialogue if it sounds too "white."

* * *

Our first day on the job, the writing staff goes to lunch with Martin. He lowers his head, makes us all join hands, and leads us in grace before we eat our meal. Moments later he's talking about women's "pussies" and wanting to "fuck somebody up."

* * *

A good mix of new writers and experienced writers, including David Wyatt — a quiet bookworm of a guy who wrote an incredibly good *Seinfeld* spec script that we bought and turned into the "dead plumber" episode; Bentley Kyle Evans (who eventually went on to create *The Jamie Foxx Show*) is a friend of Martin's who, prior to this job, has made a sizable living throwing parties at clubs he rents with a mailing list of 9,000 and invitations that read, "Martin Lawrence will be attending;" And Bennie Richburg (*The Fresh Prince of Bel Air*), who was late showing up for the first day of work because he got into trouble when he drove the Mercedes he bought from Will Smith cross-country and some cop in Georgia thought this black man stole the car from a Jew named Benny Richberg.

* * *

Jane's and my first assignment as writers is to stretch the 15-minute "presentation" episode written by John Bowman and Martin Lawrence into a full 22-minute episode. We write two "audition" scenes where we create the roles of "Stan," the radio station owner, and "Shawn," his whipping boy studio engineer, neither of which were included in the show's original presentation.

Garrett Morris from *Saturday Night Live* wins the role of "Stan." I love writing for him. We start with a sleazier version of Danny DeVito's "Louis Di Palma" character from *Taxi* and then go even sicker and weirder. Garrett is outrageously funny. Unfortunately, Martin doesn't like Garrett one bit, because he gets too many laughs. After every single script reading, Martin suggests we cut out Garrett's role.

As he continually tells us: "It's the *Martin Show,* not the Stan Show."

Jon Gries is cast as Stan's lackey at the radio station where Martin works. Martin doesn't like Jon one bit either. "Why do we need a white guy on the show? This isn't the White Guy Show. It's the *Martin Show.*"

I sense a theme.

Carl Payne is "Cole," Martin's best friend. Carl was "Cockroach," a semi-regular on the *Cosby Show*, and seems the most professional — until the first rehearsal, when he decides to ad-lib the entire script. Martin and John Bowman have a talk with him, reminding him "This isn't the Carl Payne Show."

Tommy Ford's character "Tommy" is supposed to be the educated voice of reason. We have him tell Carl's character Cole "you're stupid" (or as he says it, "you stupid"), and it gets a huge laugh. It goes into the next script, and the first of many catchphrases from the show is born.

Tichina Arnold, as Martin's foil and his girlfriend's best friend, is funny, funny, funny. She and Martin play off each other beautifully. She also has an unbelievable singing voice that I hope we can work into some episodes.

Tisha Campbell is cast as Martin's girlfriend "Gina." Tisha has an incredibly hard job on her hands, because we never know what Martin will do as we film. She is to Martin what they say Audrey Meadows was to Jackie Gleason on *The Honeymooners*. As an actress, Tisha has to go with Martin's improvisations, then figure a way to go back into the scripted lines when needed, while finding Martin sexy and funny. She's seamless. My only peeve with her is that she doesn't seem to bother to learn anyone's names. What bothers the other writers more is the size of her head. Behind her back, "pumpkin head" and "basketball head" jokes fly out of their mouths constantly.

Martin. An amazing mix of vaudeville comedian and street tough. Martin works himself hard. In addition to starring in a new series full-time, on the weekends he goes around the country doing stand-up, performing to tens of thousands of people, doing two shows a night, then flying back to work on our series — only to fly off again the following weekend and do it all again.

* * *

To Martin, it seems everything is a conspiracy. He accuses us of spelling the word "Ouija" wrong on purpose (as in, "Ouija board") in order to make a fool out of him in front of his friends when he can't pronounce it at the read-through.

We roll with it.

During our first production meeting, Martin announces there are too many white people at the table. We think he's joking until he actually makes some of us white folks stand up so the black people can sit down. John Bowman points out there are no black people attending this meeting.

"Then you better get some."

We call the Writers' Room to send us black writers who have nothing to do with the production meeting to sit in our chairs so we can stand behind them to keep Martin from storming off.

Jane comments to Martin, "You know, I'm the only woman at the table, and that doesn't seem to be a problem for anyone."

Martin glares at her from behind his sunglasses.

* * *

Adding to an already tense situation, as a stand-up comic Martin has spent years as his own director, writer, and producer. Starting a sitcom and having writers you barely know tell you what works for you and what doesn't and how your instincts are now not necessarily good can make for a rough start. It takes a while to trust that anyone's truly looking out for you other than you.

On *Martin* it's all "Martin" versus "them." And everyone besides Martin is "them."

* * *

As we rewrite a script, Bennie Richburg suggests Martin's mother say the line, "Martin! You say that to me again, and I'll slap the black off you." It's something his mother used to say to him. We laugh and put it in the script.

An hour later, when the rest of the staff has already gone home for the day, Jane and John and I get a call from the stage ordering us to "get the hell" down there. We arrive to see Martin throwing chairs, with a crazed look on his face.

"Who the fuck wrote this line? Why would my mother want to take the black off me? So I'll look like you?"

And there we are — the three "white guys" who suggested someone should take away his skin color.

The line is cut. And Martin hates us a bit more than he already does.

* * *

In an odd way, working with Martin is like working with Bob Newhart — aside from the fact that Bob doesn't say "motherfucker" four times every sentence. Martin treats his studio audiences with absolute respect. When we shoot the show, we do one take per scene and then we move on, taping the entire show in an hour and a half.

Because it's basically "live on tape" Martin earns every laugh he gets, and part of the show's success is the feeling that anything can and will happen during each episode.

* * *

One day Martin forgets his lines as he goes to compliment his character's girlfriend. Instead of stopping the scene and re-shooting, he ad-libs, "You go … girl." It's so funny and is delivered in such a completely silly way that John Bowman and I look at each other and start to laugh. The studio audience laughs, too, because Martin's intention is so adorable and "in the moment."

"You go, girl" goes into the script immediately as a scripted line and, little do we know, a national catchphrase is born. It happens quickly, too. A few months after we air, we win a People's Choice Award for Best New Series, and as presenter Whoopi Goldberg reads the nominations, someone in the audience yells, "You go, girl!" Whoopi, who I guess hadn't watched our show, seemingly has no idea what the man means and thinks she is being heckled.

Two months later, everyone in the country is saying it. It's even used on the cover of *Time*. Martin's own creation? Absolutely. Written and thought out? Absolutely not. Simply an ad-lib that sounded to us like Joe Besser — best known to my generation as the effeminate Third Stooge and "Stinky" on *The Abbott and Costello Show* on TV.

* * *

"You so crazy." "You go, girl." "Cole, you stupid." "Get to stepping." And "Whazzup!" are all "Martin" creations, as are the characters of "Momma," "Sheneneh" — a updated street version of Milton Berle's drag act, and "Jerome" — the sleazy gold-toothed "player." Jane and I add "Otis the Security Guard," "King Beef," and "Roscoe the little snot-nosed brat" to his stable of characters, and the aforementioned "Stan" and "Shawn."

* * *

As unpredictable as he is, Martin is extremely professional. We do an episode with a famous singer as a guest star. Martin and I sit around the table gabbing as the cast and crew file in for the first-day read-through. Suddenly we notice there's no guest star. (There are also no studio guys, but this doesn't seem to bother anyone.)

An hour later the singer walks in. Martin says, "Hey, man. You haven't sold that many records to show up this late." The next day the singer never shows up at all. We replace him. Martin is disgusted that anyone can be this unprofessional. I tell one of the writers that I'm surprised Martin's so calm.

"He's not calm. After work Martin plans on looking for the guy to smash his brains in with a baseball bat."

I guess that makes *two* differences between Martin and Bob Newhart.

* * *

When Martin doesn't like a script, he mumbles his lines at the first script reading and glares at the writers.

If he hates a script, he shows up wearing sunglasses, which he also wears when he's hung over. On bad days, we get sunglasses *and* a hooded sweatshirt.

Sometimes Martin barges into the Writers' Room to tell us all we have "a lot of work to do" and then pulls a few of his friends aside and threatens to kill them if they don't make the scripts funnier.

* * *

The show is a colossal success, mostly because Martin Lawrence is brilliantly funny. I love watching him perform. Yet rather than relax and trust what we're doing, Martin starts to get more and more tyrannical.

He enters the Writers' Room in his hood and sunglasses and starts screaming at me.

"What the fuck is this 'Guy' stuff?"

"I have no idea what you're talking about."

"Two lines in the script have the word 'guy' in them."

"So?"

"I don't say 'guy.' Black people don't say 'guy.' We say 'brother.' You don't fucking know this yet? How long have you GUYS been writing for me?"

* * *

We win "Best New Series" at the NAACP Image Awards. Jane and I are asked by our studio not to attend the ceremony. We not only are the co-executive producers of the show but have written most of the scripts. We're told it's nothing personal.

* * *

Martin has added to his hoodie pulled down over his face and the big black sunglasses covering his eyes when he rehearses. He now sucks on a lollipop as well. We can't see him *or* hear a word he's saying.

* * *

Getting guest stars to appear on our show is difficult. The network insists you "stunt" new shows with celebrity names. But no celebrity ever wants to do a new show, so you waste time going back and forth with lists of stars that you know won't ever do your show.

We write an episode for comedian Jon Lovitz. He passes on the offer right as we finish the script. The network insists we star a celebrity in the role anyway. I hope Martin and his friends don't know where Jon Lovitz lives.

After a long list of suggestions from the network turn us down ("How about Don Adams from *Get Smart*? Is he still alive?"), we end up with Richard Moll, who played "Bull" the bald bailiff on *Night Court*. It's suggested by the studio that we ask Richard Moll to shave his head for the one-week guest appearance so people will know who he is. And the studio rep isn't kidding.

We know we're in trouble at the read-through when Martin enters in the hoodie and the sunglasses and is, in fact, growling. He hates this script. He doesn't even finish his sentences at the read-through. He glares at the writers while he reads and shakes his head. Richard Moll's face says, "What have I gotten myself into?"

When we get to the last page, Martin storms off — five lines before the end of the script.

"This script is shit! I can't do this! I can't do this! It's a fucking cartoon!"

I wonder if he's watched any of the other episodes, where he plays his own mother with a mustache, and does snot gags for 15 minutes at a time.

"This is the *Martin* Show, not the Richard Whatever His Fucking Name Is Show."

He dictates exactly what he wants. A show where Richard Moll has no lines and Martin basically gets to beat people up. Some of Martin's ideas are inspired. This isn't one of them.

The entire script is changed. The tone of the script becomes rather dark. Except for Richard Moll's character. It's sort of like watching *Taxi Driver* with Fred Flintstone in a supporting role.

When he shows up for work the next morning, Richard Moll quits.

It seems no one delivered a script to him last night, and now he's supposed to go on camera in 10 minutes with three brand new scenes of dialogue.

John Bowman, an incredibly good show runner, persuades Richard to stay on, simply by agreeing with him when Richard says, "Martin is an asshole, and someone should knock his teeth down his throat."

Once "Bull" is calmed down, we find we're three hours behind. We decide to put his dialogue on cue cards and shoot his scenes last.

We start filming. Martin improvs that he has pubic hair in his mouth when La Wanda Page's old lady character finds her underwear in his laundry basket and swats him with it. When we ask Martin to stop, he does it longer, louder, and even more graphically. After five takes of this we decide to move on and hope we can edit it out. Martin's already getting cranky, and we're more concerned with getting the

Moll scenes before Martin, as he threatens, "puts a cap in his big white ass."

As we start the Richard Moll scenes, the audience and the cameras can see he is clearly reading off the cards and is basically reading his lines cold. Martin ad-libs on one of Richard's lines, and Richard has nothing to answer him with because it's not on the cards. Richard is about to burst a blood vessel.

We cut the cameras. Martin grabs a microphone and thanks the audience for putting up with such a slow evening: "Ladies and gentlemen, thank you for hanging in there with us. We have a very unprofessional actor working with us tonight."

Mr. Moll is professional enough not to walk out. For the remainder of the night, whenever we stop for a boom shadow or a burned-out light or a camera miscue, we hear the audience blame it on Richard Moll:

"Boo! Bull can't act! Boo!"

After the show Richard Moll leaves as fast as humanly possible. And we think twice about hiring guest stars. After all, as we've been told, it's not the "Guest Star Show."

* * *

Working on *Martin* is not easy on anyone, especially network and studio guys who are used to doing things in the usual manner. We're reinventing the sitcom with about 50% of irreverent sketch material and improv thrown into each episode. It's not so much a sitcom as it is a live-action cartoon show.

One blond, blue-eyed network boy whose looks would have done well in the Third Reich is assigned to our urban show. He doesn't get the show. He doesn't like the show. And he's always the bearer of old-fashioned studio notes that we simply ignore because they don't work on our show. One day his head explodes: "This show is shit! The president of Fox may tell you how much he loves this show to your faces, but I'm the one who has to hear what a piece of shit it is and have 12 people a day walk into my office to ask what the fuck are we doing over here?"

John immediately questions him for more details.

The young man quickly backpedals, saying how much everyone at Fox loves the show. John Bowman doesn't let it rest and pushes for more details about how much the network hates our show. The man implodes: "Fuck you all and the show... But it's a really good show. Our favorite new show, in fact." No one answers him. "Fuck you all..."

* * *

The censor and our show are a volatile mix. We can only say "ass" twice an episode and only if the mentions are spread out throughout the 22 minutes.

Most of the time, we overwrite the scripts with "damns," "hells," "asses," and dirty jokes hoping for a compromise that leaves in the one or two jokes we think are golden enough to camouflage. Inevitably, the censor cuts the wrong jokes, leaving the filthy ones behind, cutting the tame, funny ones.

The censor, a quiet little white man who doesn't know much street lingo, lets pass Martin's sleazy "player" character Jerome telling Pam he's going to "tear her up," yet we can't say "damn."

* * *

Over the weekend Martin and seven friends fly on a Lear jet to Chicago, where he had two stand-up shows to perform for 17,000 people. They are met at the airport by three stretch limos with flags, along with a marching band that plays "Hail to the Chief" as Martin deplanes. After a few moments, Martin graciously tells the greeting party that they don't have to keep saluting him.

"You've saluted enough."

* * *

Martin's stand-up gigs make editing the show difficult, because he refuses to let us send edits to the network without his approval, and he's never around to approve anything. We're forced to wait on him and his schedule for editing sessions that are all the same.

"Man, that's a good shot of me!"

"Why's the camera on Stan?"

"Bad shot of the back of my head."

"Man. They really need me in that scene..."

* * *

An added pleasure in being an executive producer is you're required to buy expensive Christmas gifts for everyone you work with. About 300 gifts. It's suggested we all chip in and buy watches with Martin's character "Sheneneh's" face on them. One writer winces at the thought of spending so much money, and I agree. These guys don't make enough.

I remember back to *Newhart* when Jane and I each had to chip in $300 each to buy presents for the actors. All we got in return was a basket of muffins from Julia Duffy and a bottle of booze from Tom Poston with dew on the bottle from when he ran out and bought it during the dinner break after receiving our gift. John agrees. The big Christmas gift will be from John, Jane, and me. Martin's manager tells us it's a nice idea, and then insists John, Jane, and I will have to pay Martin and him a piece of the action for having Martin's likeness re-created on a watch.

We decide to do keychains with the *Martin* show logo instead.

* * *

Jane and I write a Christmas show based on an incident from our theater in New Jersey.

For this *Martin* episode, we're playing a white couple in the Bethlehem scene. As we wait backstage to make our entrance, Tisha asks Jane and me: "Are you two married?" Martin looks at her likes she's insane.

"Of course they're not married. Billy's marrying ... you know, the movie star ... she does all those movies ..."

I help him out: "Adrienne Barbeau." Tisha vaguely recalls her. She admits she assumed Jane and I were married because Jane and I have the same name. Martin looks at her like she should be put in a home. I explain, "Jane's name is 'Milmore,' my name is 'Van Zandt.'"

Six months together on the show, and she never bothered to learn our names. To make up for it she tells us: "Well. You write good for the show anyway."

I tell her, "Thanks, and you act good for the lines we write you."

* * *

The Christmas episode is a big hit, and twice as funny to Jane and me because the story actually happened to us when we had a "Breakfast with Santa" calamity at our New Jersey theater back in the days before cellphones. We find ourselves with an audience full of kids and *no* Santa. We finally get through to the guy playing Santa only to find he is home and hung over and a half-hour away — with the Santa suit.

Until he can get to us, we have Mrs. Claus stall by singing Christmas songs, making up holiday stories, and as desperation hits, having all the kids in the audience try on an old sombrero she finds backstage as we cringe, hoping to God none of the kids has head lice.

When Santa finally does arrive, he has no costume — he left it at home. As an exhausted Mrs. Claus demonstrates to the kids how she can stand on her head, we quickly borrow boots from the firehouse across the street, have Santa put on red tights and a Santa hat one of the ushers is wearing, along with a red sweatshirt we find in Lost & Found. We glue cotton balls on his face to make a beard, use electrical tape for a belt, shove blankets under his shirt to make him fat, and push him out onstage.

A complete silence comes over the kids. Then we hear one kid ask, "What's wrong with him?"

Horrible experience. But a great sitcom script.

* * *

In the *Martin* episode of our story, Martin as Santa tells the story of Christmas. We get a call from the stage during rehearsals. He is refusing to say a line about the Wise Men being dressed like Winnie Mandela because it's disrespectful. Then announces he's going to play baby Jesus in the manger scene, where he'll wear a bonnet and scream, "Whazzup!"

* * *

"Thanks for our only hit."

We're at a meeting at Fox — John, Jane, Martin, and me.

Martin takes this honeymoon phase to go over our heads and sell an episode idea we already turned down because it's so tasteless: "I want to do a midget show where Tommy keeps getting beaten up by a gang of midgets, and we can make a lot of dwarf jokes and throw them around."

Incredibly, Fox gives Martin a thumbs-up.

* * *

An odd phenomenon has started. At our tapings, audience members have contests for Martin T-shirts by doing impressions of Martin's fan-favorite character "Sheneneh" — quoting detailed lines from each episode. This is incredibly too much for me to understand. We've been on the air just five weeks, yet everyone knows every inch of footage by heart.

* * *

Adrienne and I marry over the Christmas break. John Bowman asks us to only take three days for our honeymoon so I can come back and write more scripts.

We do, and when I return to the show I'm not thanked for shortening my trip. I'm yelled at by Martin again over something from an upcoming script. I have reached my limit being screamed at when we're all trying our best to make this kid a star. I have a short chat with Martin's manager.

"I've had it. If he can't talk to me or Jane with respect, we're going to walk out. I'm sorry. I don't care what I promised. Life is too short."

The manager apologizes and suddenly remembers he never sent me a wedding gift.

"Would you like a bread maker?"

"Huh? Uh … sure."

The next day I get a bread maker. Inside the bread maker I read a small card that's fallen inside. It says "Merry Christmas" to the manager and his wife.

* * *

Martin the show couldn't be bigger. More office space is confiscated from the floor to make room for Martin's "movie" people. He's a star. And now at every taping, the inevitable happens: Between takes, Martin will say something to the studio audience, and they'll laugh uproariously. Then all the executives down around the cameras will laugh hysterically as well. I ask them what Martin said, and no one knows because they didn't hear him in the first place.

* * *

In the middle of a taping, Martin drags the censor out in front of the studio audience after the man requests a line change and holds the older fellow up by the collar in front of the bleachers as he tells the audience what a lame joke he's been asked to say by "this idiot" and berates him in front of the booing crowd. The "idiot" caves, and Martin gets his way.

* * *

Martin refuses to do the Heimlich maneuver in a scene with guest-star David Alan Grier because the thinks it's "too gay." Instead he chooses to kidney punch David in the scene over and over again as the man chokes.

* * *

Martin plays a Sheneneh scene, and the only part of it I can understand is when he makes a derogatory Native American reference followed by a "whoop-whoop" sound to follow the joke. HBO president Chris Albrecht asks for another take where we can actually understand the words Martin's saying, and he asks that perhaps Martin not do the racist Native American joke. Martin goes nuts, telling Chris no one tells him how to be funny.

In view of the audience, he tells Chris to fuck himself, and starts flicking Sheneneh's fake fingernails off one by one, yanking off his wig as he tells Chris to get his boys, and that Martin will get his and they'll settle this outside.

Chris mutters, "I'm too old for this shit," gets in his car and drives away.

The rest of us follow.

* * *

Following in the footsteps of our lead actor, the other stars start to feel free to rewrite each episode to suit their egos. We arrive for a taping to find half the things we've cut in the rewrites are back in the show — put there by the actors. The show is now a free-for-all. Playing a sick person, Martin is snorting, sniffing, wiping snot on the other actors, ad-libbing dry-heave vomit jokes. It's horrible and endless. And the audience loves it.

If Martin flubs a line, he insists on picking up the line from where he blew the dialogue — seemingly unaware there are such things as camera angles that must be matched for editing. He screams that we continue because "I have other things to do." After a while, you feel sorry for him that filming his hit TV show is getting in the way of his life.

* * *

The damn midget show has arrived. We prayed it would disappear, but it's here, and it's weird.

John first has to meet with Billy Barty (president of the Little People Association) and explain our tasteless show and then find out what is acceptable and what is not. I'm hoping the meeting will end the show for good when Mr. Barty realizes that the episode is simply a 30-minute dwarf-throwing contest.

It turns out Billy Barty is fine with the subject matter. As long as we employ 30 or 40 Little People, we can toss them all night long.

* * *

Martin, who doesn't like the script that he literally dictated to us, cancels the table reading of the midget show.

"You all aren't working hard enough. You're slacking off. Must I do everything around here to save your weak material?"

John asks him not to lecture us. Martin leaves. None of us has any idea how to write this show. We kill time writing a scene where Martin thanks his writers.

* * *

Four hours later, as we finish trying to turn the script into a parable about race relations, Martin enters to tell us to throw out whatever we wrote because he came up with a better storyline where he'll get to throw more dwarfs. In addition to the gang of Little People, Martin will play a new character called Dragonfly Jones, the Master of Martial Arts — a man who happens to have a faithful assistant he'll try to kick around.

We write this masterpiece, and Martin throws out the script again: "It's not violent enough."

Two angry drafts later, we film Martin's new character, Dragonfly Jones, in his first scene. Martin has no character developed at all. He refuses to wear the makeup. He's Martin in a bald cap looking exactly like

Martin in a bald cap. He has no accent. He's not funny. He rehearses the scene on tape, basically from scratch.

Four hours and 17 characters later (yes, I'm exaggerating), we have something that's usable. The final result is Martin playing Dragonfly as some militant character who has no teeth, with "Otis the security guard's" voice. In fact, it looks a lot like Jerry Lewis's "Oriental-Guy" character — without the buckteeth, the dialect, or the craft.

The only funny moment is pure Jerry Lewis: Martin warms up for his lesson by stretching. The bit goes on for five minutes. It's funny only in its excess.

There is a famous bit of outtake footage from the silent classic *The Rink* where you see Charlie Chaplin create a masterpiece — layer by layer — as he films take after take, building the piece as he goes.

This ain't no *Rink*.

At the midget show taping, we set up big bottles of vodka on the writers' table and we all get bombed: the network execs, the HBO guys, the producers, the writers, and the censor.

We only have to reshoot one thing. When the first Little Person enters the set, he walks directly behind the couch and no one can see him.

The audience goes crazy for the show.

We all give up, pour another vodka, and watch the Little People get tossed.

* * *

The week the midgets are flying, we win a People's Choice Award for "Best New Series."

* * *

The season ends. We've sold our own sitcom to Fox and won't be coming back next season.

Tisha wishes luck to Jane and lets her know, "You and your husband's scripts were the best."

Out of the blue, Martin is sweet to us. He seeks out Jane and me, wishing us luck on our new show. What a bizarre phenomenon it has been to watch this kid grow from complete unknown to mega-star in one season of work.

He may have been difficult and demanding and out of control and a pain the ass sometimes, but I'm glad I was there to be part of it all. The guy was and is a comedic genius.

Sorry, Martin. I meant to say this "brother" is a comedic genius.

WE NEED A FAT WOMAN AND A MEXICAN

Don Rickles, Richard Lewis, and "Daddy Dearest"

"It's a go. You're official."

The president of the Fox network meets Jane and me for notes on a script we wrote.

It's about a psychiatrist who dispenses good advice but can't seem to make things work in his own love life. He lives with his politically in-correct blue-collar father, and he has a colleague who dispenses advice he doesn't take, and a neurotic brother who seems to rise above it all.

No, it's not *Frasier*. It's *Daddy Dearest,* starring our friend Richard Lewis and the legendary Don Rickles (the greatest insult comic of all time).

Both of those shows, however (*Frasier* and *Daddy Dearest*), will be debuting at the exact same time on different networks. What are the odds?

The Fox president opens our meeting with the news that Jane and I have officially sold our TV pilot, which at the time is titled *My Son the Bastard.*

"It's a go! But soften Don a little. You've probably gone too far."

We say, "sure."

"And find a different reason for Richard's wife to have left him other than being a lesbian. Coca-Cola sponsors won't buy any time if she's a lesbian."

"Um, OK!"

"Oh, and there's one more thing. The title *My Son the Bastard* isn't acceptable. But I've got a fix: How about *My Son the Fucking Bastard*?"

* * *

We fly to Las Vegas to see Don's act.

Oh, do I love Don Rickles! The greatest. Over-the-line, politically incorrect, and funnier than anyone on the planet.

"Ooh, it smells like a Mexican went bad over here."

Don introduces Jane and me from the audience, does jokes about Adrienne, and talks about our upcoming show. The audience goes wild at the idea of it.

Afterward we go backstage. Don and Jane and I chat about the show, and I suggest someone's idea of maybe Joan Rivers playing his wife in the show. He politely says, "What do we need with a *third* star?"

* * *

I arrive home to find Richard has left three rambling messages about how he needs to sit down with us and go through the script "line by line."

"If you say 'dog' and I say 'cat,' maybe we'll both come up with 'horse,' and 'horse' will be better."

* * *

The censors get hold of our first draft and inform Fox that with these kinds of jokes this script can't air before 11 p.m. We have to take out all of Richard's sexual references and all of Don's ethnic jokes. Basically, everything that makes these guys funny.

We call our studio, HBO Independent Productions, for help, but president Chris Albrecht, eager to sell a TV show, agrees with everything the network says.

We strip the script clean, turning the show into a soft sitcom that can air at 8:30 p.m. for family viewers.

Does anyone realize our show stars Don Rickles?

* * *

We're interviewing prospective casting agents. One woman suggests actors for the role of the brother. I stop her. "Oh, there's no need for that. That role is already cast."

Chris Albrecht asks: "What do you mean, Billy?"

"That's my role."

"What are you talking about?"

"I'm playing the brother role."

"What are you talking about?"

To the casting director: "Could you excuse us for a few minutes?"

* * *

On the phone with our agent. "You never mentioned we were acting in the show? That was part of the deal. You said they agreed to it."

"I, er, I never brought it up. I didn't think it would be a problem."

* * *

Chris goes to bat for us and calls Fox to see if we can act in our own show in small recurring roles, as I stand beside him. He's told, "They were hired to executive produce, not act."

That's the end of that.

It's mortifying.

* * *

The Fox president finally calls me about the "acting thing."

I explain that we're talking about literally five lines apiece. How the brother role didn't exist in the script until I wrote myself a small role.

And we wrote Jane the receptionist role because the other actors can rehearse around her when we're in the Writers' Room, since the character sits behind a desk.

He says he's grateful that we spoke and that he has no trouble with our acting in the show in recurring roles. Just not in the pilot.

I arrive home, crushed, to see Richard has called three times — with notes on the notes he already gave us.

* * *

Don, Richard, Jane, and I go to dinner at a famous celebrity haunt to celebrate that the pilot is a go. Richard and I have salads for appetizers, which turn out to be the worst possible choices. Jane and Don have soup. Ten days later, I can't walk three feet without needing to sit down, and I'm turning greenish-yellow. After collapsing on the set of *Martin*, I go to the doctor — who tells me I have hepatitis.

* * *

Jane panics at my news, not because she feels bad for me, but because, when I wasn't looking, she'd snuck a taste of my lunch with my fork. I freak out that with the script already written the network might think the show can easily go on without us. Jane finds this funny for some reason and is glad to tell anyone within earshot of my concern, including the HBO people and the network execs.

I hope she's laughing when they stick her with the gamma globulin shot.

* * *

"Richard Lewis is in the hospital with hepatitis. So you can guess what that means."

Jane asks, "We start calling Paul Reiser to take Richard's place?"

"No, it means we have to postpone the pilot for a couple of weeks."

I pretend to be upset, hang up, and go back to sleep for 22 hours a day for the next three weeks, while Jane holds the preliminary auditions, and Adrienne wakes me every six hours to stuff Chinese herbs down my throat.

The good thing is I lose a lot of weight without doing any exercise. Plus, now I can eat all the tainted shellfish I want, because apparently I can't catch this twice.

* * *

Richard stays in the hospital two weeks longer than I do and is on Demerol the entire time.

* * *

We see everyone for the role of Don's wife, "Helen" — from Polly Bergen, who refuses to read from the script but is oddly willing to take a meeting "in character," to Brett Somers from *The Match Game* and *The Odd Couple*.

* * *

Much to my delight, our soundstage is located on the original Desilu Studios lot.

Our office is silent screen legend Harold Lloyd's old dressing room: a huge five-room bungalow, with a reception area, screening room, two large offices, a steam shower, and a kitchen.

The other writers have their own offices down the hall. I joke about how big ours is to Chris Albrecht, who promises to add a Jacuzzi if we're around next season.

I hang up the famous pin-up poster of my wife in her sexy purple bustier on which she's signed, "Don't work too late," and *Daddy Dearest* is open for business — with me 14 pounds lighter and still a little greenish-yellow.

* * *

Lunch at the trendy Columbia Bar & Grill with the cast.

Carey Eidel, the tall, gangly comedian who will play the brother role, is a really nice guy. A shame I hate his guts for taking my role.

101

The always-funny Renee Taylor, who will play Don's wife, is re-served, respectful, and shy. She's sort of a big "little girl." Incredibly nice. I was hoping she'd bring her husband and writing partner, Joe Bologna, but she's alone.

Richard Lewis arrives late, in his trademark blacks, looking thin, but good. We compare yellow skin.

Don and Barbara Rickles enter last, and the show begins.

Don is on. I guess it's expected of him. Waiters and Mexican bus-boys run into the room hoping to get insulted.

"Get back in the kitchen! Jesus, they can make a million babies, but ask them to make you one sandwich! Let me make you feel at home: Immigration!"

Barbara Rickles is the perfect combination of proud wife and some-one who's seen it all before. She's very protective of Don. The only con-nection between this wife and the JAP wife from Don's act is the jewelry.

Don works the room for over two hours. We can barely eat, we're laughing so hard — well, all except for the black waiter who is not amused when Don suggests he'll be out rioting in two hours when the Rodney King verdict comes out, and an Asian woman who doesn't crack a smile. Don sees she isn't laughing, so he targets her, making Korean hooker jokes and suggesting she get her eyes fixed and "be-come one of us."

* * *

The all-important table-read of the pilot.

An audience of 20 in the bleachers, the actors at the table on the floor, and about 20 more Fox and HBO execs.

Ten minutes before we are to begin, we get a call that Renee Taylor has missed her plane, holding up everyone in the process. My first pro-fessional acting job was in Renee and husband Joe's *Lovers and Other*

Strangers. I'm honored to get to write for her. But right now I want to kill her.

We find Renee's flight number by having the casting assistant call United and pretend to be Renee to find out what connecting flight from Houston she'll be on so we can have a car pick her up in Los Angeles. The operator says the time of the flight and then (in the days before cellphones) says, "Hey, wait a minute. How are you calling us? You're in the air right now."

Click.

Renee arrives an hour and a half later.

Jane is so livid I'm afraid she's going to punch Renee in the nose when she walks in. Jane brightens only when she gets flowers from me with a card that reads: "It begins. See you in syndication."

* * *

Despite the fact I snuck back in most of Don's harder jokes, our note session consists of only one line from the network president: "This is a home run!"

Home run or not, HBO Independent Productions — the studio paying for the show — is unimpressed:

"Richard's energy is terrible."

"He has hepatitis."

"He's an actor. Can't he act like he doesn't have hepatitis?"

* * *

I love working with the president of HBO Independent Productions, Chris Albrecht. He's smart, savvy, and direct, and he doesn't take himself too seriously. He wants us to take out the climactic scene where Don interrupts Richard's therapy session and makes fun of all his patients. He is sure the network would be happier with it gone. In front of some writer friends, we tell Chris that we think he's wrong.

"Oh, so I'm wrong, am I? So, then, what am I, an asshole?"

No one answers. A long pause, then we all break into laughter. Including Chris. "Well, OK, I guess you answered my question."

* * *

The night we film the show is like a Broadway opening. Practically a black-tie event. We have a band and theater programs for the audience.

We hold the start time a few minutes. It seems one of the Pugsleys (Richard's three morbidly obese nephews on the series who dress like Pugsley Addams) is throwing up out in the alley — he ate a bowl of bananas in under two minutes right before we started the show.

The filming goes perfectly.

Don is in rare form. And he doesn't stop with the show, he attacks the audience between takes and before and after scenes.

"What are you, Irish? We need the Irish. Who else is gonna put out fires? Not the Jews. We're in the back going, 'Throw some more wood on it, Eddie.' And the black guy's going, 'Man, we're gonna get blamed for this, too.' And the Polish guy's going, 'Blamed for what?'"

* * *

After the taping, our producer catches Renee stuffing her wardrobe into her purse.

"Renee, what are you doing?"

"Billy and Jane said I could keep the costumes."

"Then why are you smuggling them out in your purse?"

* * *

Later that night in the I'm-going-straight-to-hell department: One of the Pugsleys' mothers sends her son up to me, and the obese 9-year-old says, "Billy, don't worry, I'm going to keep eating all summer, so I'll be nice and fat when we start the series in September." I fake a smile as my stomach turns.

* * *

Jane and I turn the edited show in to Fox and jump on planes for vacations. Adrienne and I go to Hawaii, staying at a place with no phones or clocks or TVs or endless faxes from Richard.

Paradise.

It's a place Chris Albrecht recommended. He'd stayed there last year, supposedly installing telephone lines and clocks and TVs at his own expense so he could do business while he relaxed.

Jane and "Richard Gere" join us for dinner on the one intersecting day when they leave the island and we arrive. The moment I see Jane's face I know she's already heard from the network. We're on the fall schedule!

The fact that this parallels Bob Carroll Jr. and Madelyn Davis learning that *I Love Lucy* was a "go" while they were also on a vacation where no one could reach them is not lost on me.

We have a nice dinner that night.

I skip the salad.

* * *

Back home in Los Angeles, I read about 50 spec scripts every day looking for staff writers. What they say is true. If a script isn't great in the first two pages, it never gets great.

To get to the good ones first, I randomly flip each script open and stick my finger in somewhere and read three lines from that spot. If I laugh, the script goes to the top of the "read" pile.

By the time we read them all, I find nine times out of 10, my finger test was correct.

Fox vetoes half the names of the experienced writers we like, because they aren't on "the approved list." I can't help thinking, "Aren't *we* the ones who have to sit in a room with these people and crank out the scripts?"

* * *

Don, Richard, Jane, and I appear at the big press kickoff in Pasadena. The four of us sit in director's chairs on a little stage while journalists from all over the country crowd into the ballroom to fire questions at us. I look out on the sea of faces, proud that our hometown papers are in the mix somewhere.

I think back to writing our first spec script, getting our first agent, consciously giving up our acting careers to become staff writers on *Newhart*, but mostly I think about growing up watching Don Rickles on *The Tonight Show* and *Dean Martin's Celebrity Roast* with my family — laughing so hard our faces hurt. Rickles was a special occasion every time he appeared. And now I get to write for him. I think of how proud Dad is.

I think about how amazing it is that Jane and I survived. Thirteen years of a marriage-of-sorts, then an ugly "divorce," a period of acting like assholes to each other, then reconciliation, then rediscovering each other as friends, then best friends. All without missing one single day of work.

We did it. We made it. It's our time.

* * *

The questions from the press begin:

"Why should anyone watch this offensive smut?"

"Doesn't it disgust you that children might see this show?"

"Do you people actually think this is funny?" Uh oh.

Don doesn't get the fact they're attacking him personally. He insults the black guy in the front row, stating how while the reporter's here, his brother is probably back in Don's hotel room stealing his cufflinks.

The questions from the papers get nastier.

I try to defend Don, explain Richard's character is there to be the politically correct one to counter Don and that's where a lot of the comedy will come from, when another reporter tells Don how his comedy is dated, politically incorrect, and offensive.

I say, "I think the millions of Don Rickles fans will disagree with you."

"'Millions?' Is that how many people fit into the seats of a Vegas show room these days?"

Richard jumps in to reiterate that for those who find Don's character politically incorrect, his character will be on hand to counter Don's opinions and put-downs, much as Rob Reiner did with Carroll O'Connor on *All in the Family.*

"You mean like when Don calls the fat lady "Shamu" and you say, 'Stop it, Dad?'"

There's no way to win this. I say: "You know, there are plenty of other shows on the air. If you don't like us, don't watch us."

The HBO people in the back of the room wince.

The next day, my words are quoted in *USA Today.*

* * *

A few weeks before we start shooting, Jane and I are summoned to offices in Century City to face a judge. It seems Richard Lewis and a writing partner wrote a script to star Richard and Don six months before we were approached by HBO to write *Daddy Dearest.* No one from HBO or Fox, nor Richard, ever mentioned this to us.

The only connection to our script is Richard and Don are in both, and they play father and son — which was the mandate from the network.

As a result, Richard and his partner are suing to be called series co-creators and share our writing credit. Richard says it's not him pushing this, it's his partner.

"And whatever happens happens."

We pretend we believe him.

Jane and I didn't know their script existed until we were served notice to appear at the arbitration.

Our lawyer says, "This is a no-brainer."

We spend all day in a Writers Guild arbitration, giving testimony on who wrote or said what, why we both had scripts that contained the "the such-and-such from hell." We explain we're writing for Richard Lewis and that's his comedy catchphrase.

The judge notes there are a few similar lines in both scripts. I say Richard pitched them to us after reading our script and to please the star of our show I put them in. Richard shrugs as if he had no idea that would make it look like we used pieces of his earlier script.

The judge asks Chris Albrecht (with Richard sitting right across from him): "Do you consider Richard Lewis to be part of the creative process on this show?"

"No, I do not."

Yow.

We return to pre-production work going over script notes with Richard the next day pretending none of this ever happened as we await the results. Jane and I have learned to compartmentalize with the best of them. So, what lawsuit?

* * *

On every sitcom, the Writers' Room is hopefully filled with brilliant people topping one another with joke after joke. Fifty percent of those jokes end up in the script, and the other 50% were said only trying to make the other writers laugh.

Offensive, inappropriate, inane jokes fill the air. You ridicule the real-life foibles of your cast, each other, news events, and pitch jokes you wish you could put in the script about cast members' egos, looks, lack of talent, personal life. It's all a way to blow off steam before you dig down and do whatever useful work you plan to get done. On *Daddy Dearest*, however, most of those inappropriate jokes go straight into the script.

Al (played by Don): "'Assume?' You know what happens when you 'assume.'"

Pete Peters (played by *Seinfeld's* Barney Martin): "Sure. You end up pulling the plug on your wife when all she really wanted was a glass of water."

* * *

The jokes quickly go off the deep end, and at one point writer Richard Vaczy (*Golden Girls*), possibly the only voice of reason in the room, says: "It's too much! It's too much! What's episode three going to be? Don and Richard flinging feces at each other?"

* * *

I call the Writers Guild to see if we won our credits arbitration from last week's hearing.

The man who answers the phone says: "Congratulations. You won! You'll share 'created by' with the people who tried to screw you out of your credit."

"Excuse me?"

"Wait. *Who* is this again?"

"Billy Van Zandt and Jane Milmore."

"Oh, sorry. Thought you were the other guys. You lost."

Click. "Created by Billy & Jane and Richard & whatever his name is."

* * *

Six weeks after we started work with the writers, the actors arrive to film the first episode.

* * *

Richard and Jane and I have hourlong phone battles over Richard's doing a Thursday pre-taping of several scenes to make the Friday night shootings easier on everyone. He also faxes us. Every night. With specific notes and random thoughts, and joke pitches, and questions about the set — and he's hilarious and I love him, but omigod!

* * *

Writers Tracy Gamble and Richard Vaczy are great assets. Tracy is a better joke guy than I am. Richard occasionally shoots his partner looks of "you can't be serious" when Tracy pitches some off-color, over-the-line joke. And he shoots him even bigger looks of disbelief when he hears me putting the same lines into the script.

* * *

Over-the-line jokes are key to this show. And every script has plenty.

Richard's mother to his father: "Oh, yeah, you're a great roommate. After living with you for two days, Anne Frank would've yelled, "Hey, boys. I'm over here!"

* * *

Every week Renee tells us she has a different agent. And she doesn't want the production assistants delivering scripts to her house, so they have to be dropped at the liquor store on the corner.

Renee is driven to and from work every day by our P.A., who tells us he thinks she steals from the craft service table.

I ask the P.A.: "Why would you think that?"

"Every time she gets out of my car, I find wilted lettuce and sliced tomatoes on my back seat."

* * *

We stupidly send the first edit of an episode over to Fox. It still needs work but is quite funny. I figure we can get their notes and integrate them into our next edit.

Fox freaks out.

Learning on the job: There is no room for imagination when dealing with the network. From here on, we add canned laughter to every edit of every episode for their viewings, and we re-edit them twice before they get the "first" untouched version.

* * *

The costumer calls. Renee keeps ripping the necklines out of her costumes to show off her cleavage. She thinks she looks nice. Don tells her she looks like a Guatemalan hooker.

* * *

Adrienne and I go to Santa Barbara for the weekend. I get a frantic call from Jane saying the president of Fox wants Monday's table-read canceled, the show shut down, and a new script written.

Jane spends her weekend salvaging what we already know is our best script — an episode done in real time, where Don goes to the DMV, a place filled with long lines, bureaucracy — and every possible ethnic group.

Precisely what the series should be.

* * *

We get our read-through as scheduled. The reading is wonderful.
No one from Fox shows up.
We call the president to tell him how well it went.
He says, "I don't care if the table reading is good, the run-throughs are good, and the taping is good. That doesn't mean it's a good show!"

* * *

"What is the story?"
These words are spoken by every studio exec after every reading of every script I've ever worked on.
"Don needs a license, goes to get a license, and gets a license. That's the story!"
"It doesn't feel like a story."
"*Seinfeld* spent an entire episode waiting for a table in a Chinese restaurant."
"Well, yes, but *that's* a story."

* * *

My favorite from *The Mothers-In-Law*, Kaye Ballard, is cast in our show as the DMV woman from hell. Kaye corners me, "Thanks for bringing me back to TV."

Most of the kids on our staff don't know who she is — they're too young to have seen her work. Someone from the network asks if we should use her. "It might look like a rerun."

But after the table reading, everyone's pitching, "How about Kaye comes back and dates Barney?" "What if Kaye and Renee are best friends?" "Can't Kaye move in next door?"

* * *

At the DMV show taping, we finally get to show the series' potential with Richard and Don doing Richard and Don at their very best.

No one from Fox shows up.

* * *

The following episode, guest star Angie Dickinson (*Police Woman, Dressed to Kill*) quits after reading the script.

"Was it a problem with the joke about how the starving kids in Somalia could solve their hunger problems if they'd just eat all those flies?"

"No. Apparently in the seduction scene, it calls for her to come out in a negligee."

I change the costume to a sexy dress.

She agrees to do the show.

And the tasteless fly joke kills.

* * *

The tug of war between the "Don Rickles Show" we want to write and the "Kindly Grandfather Show" the network wants us to write continues. But we keep fighting. Ours is the right show for Rickles.

The Fox folks hold an impromptu testing session in Burbank to show us with written proof that the DMV show and all shows like it will be a failure. The pilot and the DMV show are the big hits of the night. These are the kinds of shows the audience says "they want to see more of."

The next day the Fox president looks at the results and says, "What do those tests know — they're just people off the street."

Can't get a break.

* * *

Frank Sinatra has agreed to appear on the show.

But he can't shoot the scene until next Monday "sometime between noon and 7 p.m." That is, "… if he feels like it when he wakes up."

* * *

Rambling nightly faxes continue from Richard Lewis with notes and joke pitches on the upcoming scripts. Sent to the offices at 2 a.m., 4 a.m., 6 a.m., five days a week. And to our house. It's become a running joke with Adrienne and me to see how often we can fool around without hearing the fax machine go off.

* * *

Monday, we keep getting updates throughout the day as we sit in the Writers' Room.

"Mr. Sinatra is still asleep."

"Mr. Sinatra is in the shower."

"Mr. Sinatra is eating breakfast."

And finally, "Mr. Sinatra is in the car."

At 4 p.m., Mr. Sinatra finally shows up. He spends a total of 3 minutes and 28 seconds — between getting out of his car and driving away. We know, because it's on the time code. I walk into the absolutely silent soundstage seconds behind him. His costume is whatever he has on. The cameras silently start rolling.

Mr. Sinatra looks around at the set and says: "You got nine minutes. What do I do?"

Don says, "Nothing, just stand there, we'll put a camera on you and hope to God you're not drooling all over yourself."

Frank is shown to his mark, rehearses once, reading the lines off a cue card, shoots it once and then heads for his car.

"The things you do for friends!"

That's 3 minutes and 28 seconds.

As the car pulls out, I hear him tell his driver: "One hour door to door. Not bad. We should get into this TV business."

Jane runs onto the set. "Where is he?"

"Where were you?"

"I wanted to fix my lipstick. Where is he?"

"By now? Pulling into his driveway."

* * *

Richard, living in his own world, submitted a long list of specific photos he wanted taken with Mr. Sinatra. Both to pose in Richard's trademark "The Scream" pose. Both posing like the cover of Frank's "Come Fly with Me" album. Some with Don. Most without.

The only shot we get is Sinatra walking between Don and Richard to get to his car.

* * *

We're told by the network that Jane may not play Richard's ex-wife in next week's show. Fox's orders are to "concentrate on the writing." We cast Leann Hunley from *Days of Our Lives* instead. It's clear they are never going to be OK with us performing. Our acting careers go into another box. We'll learn to be content with acting in our plays.

* * *

Richard does *The Howard Stern Show* to publicize our show. Howard is ruthless, making fun of Richard and all the older guest stars we keep using. (I keep casting my comic idols from when I was a kid.)

He asks why we don't cast sexy, hot babes instead. He asks, "Who are you having on next? Imogene Coca? Rose Marie?"

It's a funny interview. But I turn around and immediately cancel the scheduled plans to use, yes, Imogene Coca and Rose Marie.

* * *

Our "Halloween" episode. Don takes his little grandson out trick-or-treating and returns with the wrong kid, a little black kid in the same Ninja Turtle costume as his grandson. It might as well be an episode of *Full House*.

* * *

The last in the "kindly grandfather-series" of scripts was originally pitched and approved as "Don, Richard, and Barney go fishing out on the ocean." The HBO guys love this because they bought a boat for their series *Down the Shore* and since the show got canceled, it sits on blocks in a warehouse. The week before we film, we're told it can't take place on the ocean because it's too expensive. We're instructed to have the cast fish off a pier — on our soundstage — with a cloudless blue sky behind them, no birds, and offstage water.

The script lies there on the table.

And, again, after the first run-through, the network exec tells me, "It isn't funny."

"No kidding. I've been telling you these soft, kindly grandfather shows don't work for us. Maybe now you'll understand."

"What can we do?"

"Let Rickles be Rickles."

"You're right. You're right. There's only one way to fix this script. We need a fat woman and a Mexican!"

* * *

The next day after the addition of, yes, a Mexican and a fat lady, Don says, "What happened?" You turned a drama into a funny script!"

I thank him and walk away. He calls after me: "There he goes, everyone. The man that got us into 66th place in the ratings."

* * *

I get a call in the Writers' Room — a rare thing, because I don't like to be disturbed when we're working.

"Billy, can you please talk to the costumer? She's ready to quit."

"Why?"

"One of the actresses wants the costumer to pull her pantyhose up and down when she uses the ladies' room because she doesn't want to ruin her nails."

I hang up the phone and turn back to my partner.

"Jane ... you're wanted on the set."

* * *

We receive two bottles of champagne from Fox. The card says, "Thank you for your hard work." Jane and I look at each other.

"Maybe they simply appreciate how hard we work?"

"I think we were supposed to get canceled, and somebody's secretary screwed up. Just in case, I'm not calling to thank anyone."

* * *

We have a serious meeting with the studio about what to change for the back nine episodes if we should get the go-ahead to do more. It's decided to eliminate Richard's doctor office set. We'll only go back there occasionally for office-driven storylines—e.g., a planned episode guest-starring Jerry Lewis as a lunatic patient who won't leave Richard alone, etc.

Otherwise, the show will be a domestic comedy that starts in the living room and gets us out into different arenas—e.g., the upcoming jail show, the casino show, the DMV show, an upcoming airplane show.

Leann Hunley will be featured more often as Richard's ex-wife, as will Alice Ghostley (*Bewitched, Designing Women, Captain Nice*) as

"Crazy Aunt Adelaide" (a nod to my mother's sister), and we'll have revolving hot young girlfriends for Richard — as was originally intended, of course. We map out the exact stories we want to do and in which order, assigning Jane and me to write one out of every three scripts.

* * *

The promos for the upcoming Sunday night show not only include the entire two-sentence cameo by Sinatra, but they've arranged the footage to make it look like Adrienne (who is guest-starring) is Sinatra's girlfriend and he's the big mob boss the entire episode revolves around, instead of Alex Rocco (Moe Green from *The Godfather*).

Screw it. If people tune in, they'll be happy with what they see, anyway.

* * *

We've now taken to showing as much as two minutes of outtakes at the end of each episode. And sometimes they're funnier than the episodes themselves, because when Don lets loose, he's unstoppable.

* * *

The jail episode is my absolute favorite. Exactly what the show should be.

The only network note: "As usual, too many sodomy jokes."

I bet *Full House* never gets that note.

* * *

We're asked to let guest-star Andre Rosey Brown go because Martin Lawrence doesn't want us "stealing" actors who have also guest-starred on his show. It was bad enough this show stole Jane and me.

Garrett Morris plays a version of his character "Stan" from *Martin* on our show this week, as well. He tells me this is the most he's gotten to do as "Stan" this season. Sadly, Jane and I used to write all the Stan dialogue on Martin and, in my opinion, none of the other guys still on staff quite understand Stan, which I'm sure had something to do with it. It's a shame, because he's so funny. He can always move next door to Don and Richard. Right next to Kaye Ballard.

* * *

Guest star Huntz Hall (of *The Dead End Kids* and later *The Bowery Boys*) arrives in a big, green, rusted-out Cadillac — an old man in a thrift-shop-looking raincoat who lives in the Valley and negotiated his own deal.

This is a great thrill for me. Every Sunday after church, my brother and sister and I would walk the three blocks to my grandparents' house for Sunday Dinner. As Nana cooked, we'd sit in the living room and watch Bowery Boys movies on Channel 5. Huntz Hall's character "Satch" was one of my comic heroes.

As soon as the reading ends, the Fox executives immediately ask me to replace him.

"He's old. He'll never learn it. Replace him."

I ask, "Can we rehearse with him once?"

After the next run-through — where he's off-book and hilarious, the Fox people ask him to guest-star in an upcoming pilot.

* * *

At Friday's pre-shoot, Richard asks for nausea pills, then for oxygen to be brought to the set. Then he wants a doctor. We learn that Richard's blood pressure is sky high. We finish the scene — and Richard goes to the hospital.

I refuse to shut down the shoot night. I want this show in front of an audience tonight. It's our best one yet, and Richard's screwing it up by not being here. We hold the audience an hour and a half, with a P.A. at the hospital by Richard's side calling us with updates every 10 minutes. The studio audience views the "Atlantic City Show" and the

"DMV Show" unaware that our star is across town in a hospital gown hyperventilating into a paper bag.

The P.A. calls from the hospital. Richard is suffering an anxiety attack. But because there is a history of heart disease in his family, the doctor won't take a chance and will hospitalize him for the night. The shoot is called off. Don graciously does an hour of his nightclub act with the crowd, and everyone goes home happy.

* * *

Sunday afternoon Jane and I meet at the Bungalow and watch the first cut of what we pre-shot during the day on Thursday and Friday and hope we have enough footage to piece the episode together without re-shooting any of it in front of an audience. Director Howard Storm and editor Tony Hayman do a great job putting it together. No need for re-shoots.

* * *

The day after the jail show airs, in which Don tells a flasher "Oh, I see what Hervé Villechaize left you in his will," our assistant buzzes me.

For those too young to remember *Fantasy Island*, Hervé Villechaize played Tattoo, the Little Person sidekick to Ricardo Montalban's Mr. Roarke. Every episode opened with Tattoo pointing at the sky and yelling, "The plane! The plane!" to welcome the *Fantasy Island* guests.

"Billy, Hervé Villechaize's widow is on the phone for you."

"I'm not taking that call."

"What do I tell her?"

"Whatever you want."

A short while later, our assistant buzzes me.

"Mrs. Villechaize said to tell you you're heartless, your joke was disgusting, and that her husband was hung like a horse, so it wasn't even accurate."

* * *

Our Thanksgiving show.

Everything clicks. Our show has hit its stride. Unfortunately, it's 10 shows too late and nobody at the network cares. After the rewrite, Jane leaves to run errands for her upcoming wedding on Saturday.

I get a call from Chris. "How long are you going to be there?"

He won't tell me what the news is, but he doesn't say, "Break out the champagne."

He arrives, parks his car, and walks in.

"The show is going on temporary hiatus. We have until December 15 for Don's option to run out, so we have to be told we're canceled or picked up by then."

I'm not surprised. Once they start dropping your promos, don't show up at tapings, and send you champagne with "thanks for your hard work anyway" notes attached, you can sort of tell whether they're behind you. (They're not.)

Chris says he wants the last three shows finished as soon as possible and sent over to Fox in the hope we can change their minds.

I doubt it matters.

* * *

"It was never the show we bought," is the quote. I still don't understand what that means. They bought a show called *My Son the Bastard* starring insult comic legend Don Rickles.

The only shows that weren't what we promised were the four pieces of fluff they made us do: "The Bully Show," "The McDonald's Show," "The Fishing Show," and "The Halloween Show."

Not that they weren't funny. They were fantastic. But the other ones were better.

I get to call Jane, four nights before her wedding, and tell her she's unemployed. I also call the actors. Renee takes it badly. Now she'll only star as a series regular in two network TV shows at the same time instead of three (*Dream On* and *The Nanny*). Three had to be a record.

Don doesn't understand why we were canceled, and I can't give him a reason. It doesn't make sense. The ratings are great, and the fan base is huge.

The next day, we gather our cast and crew family. They already know what's coming. I officially give them the news. I apologize if Jane and I are the cause. Then I wish them a good rehearsal — we still have two shows to film despite the pink slip.

* * *

That afternoon, the Fox show *Bakersfield* gets picked up. Number 88 out of 89 shows on the airwaves. Our producer Frank Pace keeps muttering "cocksuckers" over and over like a mantra.

* * *

Don is suddenly more relaxed on the set. We should've been canceled weeks ago. No pressure on him now, I guess.

* * *

Jane's wedding is fabulous.

Don, the sweetest man in the world, does a 15-minute toast/stand-up routine honoring Jane, her husband, their parents, and Adrienne and me in the process. Renee wishes Jane good luck.

"May you be as happy as Joe and me. After all these years, we're still hot for each other."

Jane thanks her.

"It's true, you know. We do it on the kitchen table. On the floor. In the dressing room…" We know about the dressing room. Anyone within earshot knows about the dressing room.

* * *

Fox picked up *Roc*. Number 87 out of 89 shows on the airwaves.

* * *

Frank Pace and I finalize the edit for the Thanksgiving episode hoping that once Fox sees it they'll change their minds. It's our best show.

Jane and I act in the final show. Screw it! What can they do to us now? My scene in a restaurant is pre-shot during the day so I can watch the rest of the show on the monitors with my producer hat on at night.

Renee comes early to watch. "You're funny!" One extra keeps ruining takes because she can't stop laughing at my maitre d's lisping Portuguese accent. We also hire Andre Rosey Brown back for a bit with Renee in the hospital scene.

* * *

As we shoot the final episode, there are lots of jokes from Richard and Don every time we ask for another take.

Richard: "What for? It's over."

Don: "I'm sorry I blew the line, but, hey, I learned the lines for 13 weeks and where did it get us?"

* * *

The crew thanks me for a fun and easy work environment. The writers thank us. I hate putting all these people out of work. Everybody is sad, but the mood isn't somber. A "Let's show everybody what we're made of" mood permeates the set.

Another of my comic heroes, Howie Morris (Uncle Goopy from Sid Caesar's *Your Show of Shows* and Ernest T. Bass from *The Andy Griffith Show*), steals the show as the dying old man in the hospital whose tubes Richard and Renee keep accidentally sitting on.

The audience goes wild for the final gag where Richard looks behind the hospital curtain to see Don and Renee in bed together, reunited. I had hoped this scene would take place in year five, but if this is the last show, I want the characters to have closure.

* * *

The wrap party is terrific. But nobody comes from Fox or HBO.

Don corners Jane and me at the end of the night and asks us not to give up on the show, fight for it, and to call Fox daily. And if we're canceled, please find out why. He wants to know if it's him.

* * *

Finally we walk back to the office, Jane and I — the first to show up last April, and now the last to leave. We slowly strip down the walls, empty files, and throw out scripts.

For such a loud show, it ends quietly.

* * *

They pre-empt us the following week with a night full of *Simpson's* reruns. The following week we're officially canceled. On my birthday.

The episode Jane and I acted in doesn't air.

Daddy Dearest — still the best job I ever had. Why? Don Rickles. Honored to work with him. Proud to be his friend. And I never laughed so hard in my life.

WHITE PEOPLE SMELL LIKE BALONEY

The debut of the WB Network and "The Wayans Bros."

Shawn and Marlon Wayans have been given their own television show. At this point in their careers they are only known as the brothers of comedians Keenan and Damon Wayans. This is akin to giving Zeppo and Gummo Marx their own show, and hoping they're as funny as Groucho and Harpo.

Jane and I get a phone call from David Janollari, VP of Comedy at Warner Bros. Studio, asking us to take over *The Wayans Bros.* as show runners six weeks before it is set to air.

I ask: "What happened to the old show runner?"

"Oh, he's been fired."

"Why?"

"Let's just say the show goes on the air six weeks from today, and after six months no one's even seen a script."

"David, we can't break stories, write scripts, cast series regulars, shoot a show, and edit in six weeks."

The reply: "Sure you can. You write fast. And you won't be alone. There is a staff of accomplished writers waiting for you over there. Some of the best in the business."

Jane looks at me hopefully.

"And since you're debuting in January, it'll only be 13 episodes tops. And you'll be part of history as the first show to ever air on the WB Network."

I picture the kinescope of Bob Hope doing his first NBC television monologue in that historical piece of footage, and I wonder how cool it would be to have written and produced it.

"The first show, huh?"

* * *

Within the hour, without a deal in place or a speck of material read, we are ushered onto the Warner Bros. Ranch in Burbank to take over the show. We go up a large, rickety flight of metal stairs and into the ugliest office suite I've ever seen — peeling paint, no light, stained carpets. I can tell no one has faith in this show; otherwise we'd be in the good offices downstairs. At the least they would have gotten what looks like blood out of the rug.

We walk into an office where we meet Shawn and Marlon. They stare, unsure of what to make of us. They're at a table with their manager and one other man, who asks: "Can I help you?"

"Hi, we're Billy Van Zandt and Jane Milmore. We're the new show runners."

A pause, then the "old" show runner asks:

"The new *what*?"

As the "old" show runner calls his agent to confirm he has, in fact, been fired (by us, apparently!), we call David Janiollari to scream. The voice on the other end laughs like a little kid.

"You better get off the phone. You only have six weeks to get a show on the air."

David's so good at his job I'm equally impressed at how he can manipulate us and appalled that we're such suckers.

* * *

We enter the conference room to meet our staff of "accomplished writers." A sea of eager, smiling faces looks up at us. There are hundreds of them, or so it seems. No one looks older than 18. I look at the calendar and realize I don't have time to see how well any of these people write or to even try to teach them. Too many voices in the room will slow us down.

To save time, I fire them all. Basically, "Get in the car, the lot of you."

* * *

As the writers pack their belongings, Jane and I enter our predecessor's office and pick up the stack of "finished" scripts sitting on the desk — all three of them — and start reading. The three scripts are for completely different series ideas. There's not even a premise for this show. Jane and I shut the door and realize we'll have to create a brand-new series on our feet with only two mandates — it goes on the air in six weeks. And it stars Zeppo and Gummo.

* * *

Shawn and Marlon tell us what they want — an irreverent show that blends outrageous sketch material with a traditional sitcom, as we did on *Martin*. We decide to write a version of *The Honeymooners*. Shawn will be our Ralph Kramden, a good-hearted soul with big dreams that always backfire; Marlon will be our Ed Norton, the sidekick who always gets him into more trouble. We throw in an upper-class girlfriend (the Alice Kramden role) so Shawn has someone to dream big for, and the already-cast comic John Witherspoon becomes their crazy father, Pops, who owns the diner where they all work. (No *Honeymooners* connection for him at all, sorry.)

We scribble up "sides" (audition scenes) in an hour, so we can audition and cast the leading lady for a show that is still unwritten.

* * *

To save us writing time and to satisfy the stars as well, we bring Shawn and Marlon into the Writers' Room to work on the scripts with us. They are hilarious. Thank God. But almost everything they pitch is an "ass joke." Funny, but still an "ass joke."

However, they fit in with our small staff of new writers, unlike most actors in a Writers' Room who cause your work to stop dead, as they expect everything they suggest to be brilliant.

Shawn has leading-man looks and does a near-perfect Denzel Washington impression that we work into a script.

Marlon is an amazing physical comedian, with a penchant to undress for laughs as often as humanly possible — which Jane is less than thrilled with. He also does an impression that puts Shawn on the floor with laughter every time. I have no idea who it's supposed to be.

It turns out it's me.

With Shawn and Marlon in the Writers' Room, we're able to try out bits to see if they work before we finish writing them. It saves a lot of time. It's eye-opening, too.

Me: "We need a list of WASPY white guy things for this joke to work."

Shawn suggests: "How about if I call him a martini-drinking, baloney-smelling…"

Me: "Baloney what?"

Shawn: "Baloney-smelling. All white guys smell like baloney."

A pause, then he adds: "Except you."

* * *

Shawn and Marlon want appropriately irreverent opening credits. We're told to give them what they want. And that's what they get. The storyline has Shawn and Marlon sporting afros and Jimmie ("J.J.") Walker *Good Times* clothes, singing a deliberately offensive TV theme with lyrics like, "We're happy and we're singing and we're colored," and it ends with a bus smashing into an old lady crossing the street.

* * *

We call David. The show is slipping away from us.

At the run-through I ask, "You sure this is what you want?"

He says: "It's incredible. It's edgy and it's in-your-face!"

* * *

We find out Warners can't give Jane and me a show royalty — a common practice for every show runner. It's a weekly fee for every show produced (even after you leave the job) for creating and developing the series. This show has been in development for a while, and there are too many people who preceded us taking royalties.

So instead, when we film the opening credits, I give myself a voiceover line as the off-camera director. "Cut. Print. Beautiful, guys."

Spoken under a union contract, I get paid VO money for every episode produced. Better than nothing.

* * *

We scrape together a few "irreverent" story ideas, get them approved by the network, and start writing.

- An "Afro Cab" episode, where the boys run a taxi service that caters exclusively to "The Brother Man" and not "The Other Man."

- An airline episode, where Marlon can't get through security without stripping naked and riding the X-ray machine, where it's discovered he ate a metal Hot Wheels car when he was little.

- "Brazilla" — a spoof of *Godzilla* movies, where Shawn and Marlon go in to the kiddie-party business and end up performing at a Japanese architectural firm, the result of which is screaming Japanese kids running for their lives as competing kid-show entertainers in dinosaur suits fight amongst the office building mockups.

* * *

We call David.

Again, I ask. "Are you sure this is what the network wants?"

Again, same answer: "Trust me. It's in-your-face. It's urban. It's now."

* * *

Sets are being built, production meetings are happening every two minutes, and each writer gets assigned an episode and is given one week to write it.

Before Jane and I can start writing ours, an irate woman screams at me on the phone. I have no idea who she is. We're juggling so many balls I barely know my assistant's name.

I guess I overstepped the key makeup woman's authority when our leading lady called to ask for a different makeup lady from the one she tested with the day before and, preoccupied with getting the scripts ready, I said yes. I listen as the woman screams at me at the top of her lungs. When she's done, I fire her.

For all I know, she never leaves the lot and we use her for the rest of the season.

* * *

The first shoot day. Shawn and Marlon are two hours late. They were up all night having twists put in their hair.

One person who is on time and ready to work is guest-star Gary Coleman, who takes every two minutes to ask me to create a new show for him.

* * *

I sit in the bleachers waiting for our stars, when I see an old lady sitting amongst the extras.

"I'm Billy."

"I'm Shirley."

I find out this 90-year-old lady still lives by herself and works around town as an extra to make ends meet. The thought of this woman hustling for jobs and traipsing all over town to make $50 a day kills me. I make Shirley Greene a permanent customer at "Pops' Diner," where she'll work as long as we're on the show.

* * *

We film the first episode: "Goop, Hair It Is." It's a Wayans version of the classic "Chef of the Future" episode of *The Honeymooners*.

Shawn and Marlon invent pomade called "Goop, Hair It Is." They go on live TV to promote it with guest-star Gary Coleman, and all hell breaks loose when the stage lights set the pomade on fire, resulting in Gary Coleman's head going up in flames and Shawn and Marlon beating him to death as they try to put them out.

The big special effect is when the guys' heads start smoking. It's decided by the special effects man that the best way to do this is to blow cigarette smoke through long tubes worn under their wigs.

No one bothers to tell us is that Shawn is asthmatic.

We film the scene. Shawn starts to choke—seemingly to death. He turns green and falls down.

Marlon says Shawn has a few more takes in him and that we should do it again.

* * *

As we film in front of the audience, Marlon and Shawn decide it's funny to ad-lib their lines like Stepin Fetchit or like Buckwheat from the *Little Rascals*, much as the older Wayans brothers used to do on their sketch show, *In Living Color*.

"Hello, li'l Gary Colemanz."

"That's ri-squisite." (Instead of "that's exquisite.")

The studio audience thinks it's the funniest thing they've ever heard. We ask the brothers to stop. They promise they will, then do even more of it on the next take. We get a thumbs-up from the studio people and move on.

* * *

Garrett Morris (also playing himself) is guest-starring straight from his well-publicized stint in a hospital after being shot getting his car washed in a sketchy area in Downtown L.A.

Shawn ad-libs: "Come on in, Mr. Morris. Don't worry, we won't shoot you."

The studio audience screams and stomps its feet. The Warner Bros. execs nod at us vigorously.

* * *

Marlon in a "before" segment of his infomercial sits crooked in a wheelchair looking like one of the worst-off of Jerry's Kids, and then, after he's used "Goop, Hair It Is" is miraculously able to run in fast speed and shoot baskets.

The studio audience, the studio, and the network execs shriek with laughter. I think we've lost our minds.

* * *

The show debuts. It's not quite the Bob Hope footage I'd hoped for.

The Los Angeles Times says Jane and I have "set the black race back 200 years." A meeting is called by Warner Bros. to tell us we've tarnished the image of the WB.

* * *

Jane and I leave after our contracted 13 episodes. The show runs for five seasons and goes on to eternal life in syndication, where it plays somewhere every single day. It makes Marlon and Shawn huge stars and opens the door to highly successful movie careers.

Who knows? If given the chance, Zeppo and Gummo could have been big, too.

CAN HE LOOK LESS JEWISH?

"Staten Island, 10309"

Sometimes you do everything right.

It was the fastest sale we ever made. We literally say the words, "*Seinfeld* for teenagers," and CBS buys the show on the spot.

CBS is determined to find a younger audience this season.

We write the script in less than a week and turn it in to the studio despite pleas from our agent. ("Don't ever let them know you write fast.") Instead of an excited call that says, "Let's film it!" we are told that the show is now "cast contingent" because the 15-year-old we wrote it for has been shifted into a different CBS project in the seven days we were writing the script.

"But if you can find another great 15-year-old kid with the comic timing of Rodney Dangerfield, we'll be happy to make your show."

We see what seems like every kid in the world. They all stink. Our friend Nancy Carson, one of the most successful children's agents in the business, sends us videotape. She's been pushing this kid David Krumholz on us for over a year. After discovering him in a high school play, she signed him and got him on Broadway with Judd Hirsch in *Conversations with My Father*. We watch the tape. His timing is impeccable.

Warner Bros. signs him to a holding deal. CBS loves him. It's a go.

Except now it's a "presentation," not a "pilot." The difference: Filming with a $300K budget versus a $1M budget and hoping our cheaply made presentation can compete against all the other slick-looking $1M budget pilots when the network president picks his next season.

Suddenly the funny scene in the school bus that opens the show has to be rewritten to take place by the school's front door — we can't afford a bus. Otherwise, thanks to our great producer Frank Pace and a lot of favors, everything will look exactly the way we'd want it even if the budget were three times what we've got to work with.

As the battle-ax teacher, we cast Kaye Ballard over the phone — slipping the role in as a guest star instead of a series regular to avoid making her go through the casting approval ritual for all series regulars. Andrew Leeds and Ashley Levitch become our "George and Elaine" to David's "Jerry," and we round out the cast with Dana Baron from *Vacation* and newcomer Becky Herbst, whose mother circles the poor girl like a shark to ward off the boys (and, I suppose, the grips).

The table-read of the script is spectacular. Everyone scores. I wish we had a camera to film on the spot. It doesn't sound like we have more than three jokes to fix.

Some great friends have come by to help us with the rewrite. Alan Kirschenbaum (*Coach* and later *Yes, Dear*) in a loud voice asks the president of Warner Bros. if he can buy into the back end since it's going to run forever — and he did it across the room to show the network his approval. (Thank you, Alan.)

We get no notes at all. Well, one. From Warner Bros. to our director: "Don't fuck it up, Joel." And we're done.

Kaye Ballard has become an issue with CBS and me, because they wanted to cast a "hip, young" teacher. But we wrote the role for Kaye. Some guy I never saw before in the prior six-month process says, "Kaye Ballard? I just don't see the teacher role that way." And then other CBS people I've never met start to agree with him. I hold my ground.

133

The run-through the next day is great. Feels like the old days at *Daddy Dearest* when I loved every second of going to the studio.

Our favorite writer/friends Alan Kirshenbaum, Eric Gilliland (*Roseanne*), Lloyd Garver (*Family Ties* and *Home Improvement*), Peter Noah (*Anything But Love* and eventually *West Wing* and *Scandal*), John Bowman (*Martin* and *The Hughleys*), Bruce Rasmussen (*Roseanne* and *The Drew Carey Show*), Matt Ember (*The Wayans Bros.* and eventually the movies *Failure to Launch* and *Get Smart*), Tracy Gamble and Richard Vaczy (*Golden Girls*), and Greg Malins (eventually *Friends* and *Will and Grace*) are all there to root us on and help us punch up afterward.

CBS is impressed with our crew and says: "This would be the most expensive room in town — if you were paying them — and you don't even need them. There's nothing to do." One note from CBS, "Keep an eye on Kaye in case 'we' have to replace her," and they're gone.

None of my writer friends has notes. When I tell them about CBS's concerns over Kaye, in unison I hear: "Fuck them. She's great."

After the run-through, the rewrites are quickly done, and then a four-star catered meal is offered to the friends who were kind enough to show up. Matt Ember asks me if he is "the only writer in this room who isn't making a million dollars a year." I say, "Yes" and he looks sad for the rest of the night. After we're finished stuffing ourselves, everyone (including Jane and me) will head off to see a run-through of Bruce Helford's *Drew Carey Show* pilot back at Warners' main lot.

Two days later, *Staten Island 10309* films as smoothly as a show in its 10th season. Great laughs. The biggest laughs are, of course, from David Krumholz — everything he does is funny — and from Kaye Ballard. God bless her (and screw you, CBS guy).

The usual studio panic sets in between takes, with unnecessary acting notes and camera angle suggestions flying fast and furious. Jane is in the greenroom with the network/studio people with a direct telephone line to me on the stage, where I'm positioned next to the cameras. Jane calls me after each take with studio executive notes.

Billy and Lucille Ball on the set of *Life With Lucy*

With Laura Stannard in *The Old Bird Sanctuary in the Park Trick (And I Fell For It)*

Billy and Jane 1975

Neil Simon's *Star Spangled Girl* with Jane

Love, Sex, and the I.R.S.

Newhart with Peter Scolari

Anything But Love

With Jamie Lee Curtis

Father Van Zandt on *Sydney*

Bob Carroll Jr, Madelyn Davis, David Steinberg on the set of *I Love Lucy: The Very First Show*

The cast of *Do Not Disturb*, taken before the script was written (clockwise from L: Sally Winters, Drew Hollywood, BVZ, Sherle Tallent, Glenn Jones, Jane) - Jane is in a costume for a sketch we never wrote. (Photo Credit: Danny Sanchez)

Drop Dead with Jonathan D. Mack and Jane Milmore

Backstage at *Drop Dead* – that's not Tina Louise

With Martin Lawrence

Daddy Dearest with Don Rickles and Richard Lewis

With Huntz Hall

The cast of *Staten Island 10309* (Back row: Jane, Kaye Ballard, BVZ. Front row L to R: Andrew Leeds, David Krumholz, Ashlee Levitch, Dana Barron)

Bless This House with Cathy Moriarty and Andrew Dice Clay

Olympia Dukakis and Penny Marshall

Adrienne with Walker and William

The Hughleys with DL and Jane

Off-Broadway in *Silent Laughter* with Art Neill (Photo Credit: Martha Swope)

The cast of Off-Broadway's *You've Got Hate Mail* (L to R: Fran Solgan, BVZ, Glenn Jones, Jane, Barbara Bonilla) (Photo Credit: Danny Sanchez)

Merrily We Dance and Sing

The original cast of *The Boomer Boys Musical* - still touring! (L to R: Tom Frascatore, Jeff Babey, BVZ, Glenn Jones) (Photo Credit: Danny Sanchez)

Teresa and me - in Warsaw, Poland with the cast of *Love, Sex, and the I.R.S.*

The Siblings: Kathi and Steven (Photo Credit: Shevett Studio)

My stepson Cody, living in Japan when he's not composing in Los Angeles

Teresa (Photo Credit: Annie Wood @anniewoodworld)

Walker and William

Billy and Jane (Photo Credit: Danny Sanchez)

Produced by
BILLY VAN ZANDT
&
JANE MILMORE

End Credits

Every time she calls I tell her to tell them to go to hell and leave us alone, and she pretends I said something else and tells the network/studio people that I said I'll "see what I can do." She yells at me later when everybody is gone.

At one point, between takes, we are asked if we can make David Krumholz look less Jewish.

We're done in an hour and a half, pickups included. Then we all go off to punch up *The Drew Carey Show* pilot.

* * *

The in-house testing the next week is going along great until Jane nicely tells the guy running the test that this is all a waste of time, and that if testing worked at all, every show on TV would be a hit.

As true as this is, this was not the time to tell the guy.

Suddenly he goes from loving our show to despising our show. His questions suddenly turn sour, making anyone who liked our show feel stupid for liking it. Regardless, we test "above average." Or as you hear it from every writer with a pilot, we "tested through the roof!"

In all the years I've been doing this I never heard of one pilot that didn't test "through the roof." I've noticed, though, that no one ever tells you how low the roof is.

Everybody's high on this one going. Me especially. I'd love to work on this for 10 more years. I love the cast. I love the crew. I love writing for this show.

The fall TV schedule is announced. We're not on it. Jane isn't surprised at all. "As soon as we got the note about David looking too Jewish, I knew we were dead." CBS tells us a midseason replacement is a possibility — which is what they tell everyone, instead of saying you didn't make it. Every pilot tests "through the roof," and every pilot not on the fall schedule is being "considered for midseason."

And sometimes doing everything right just isn't enough.

A TOUCHY SITUATION

Andrew "Dice" Clay, Cathy Moriarty, and "Bless This House"

It's shoot night of the first episode of a brand-new series. Jane and I enter the soundstage to see our star refusing to put on his character's costume because, "only fags wear postal uniforms." Our leading lady is bitching that her co-star doesn't know his "fucking lines." And two men named "Hot Tub Johnny" and "Club Soda Kenny" are standing behind our star with a towel and his script — fresh from their afternoon jobs of handing him his weights at the gym.

Just another day on *Bless This House* with Andrew "Dice" Clay.

* * *

Writer Bruce Helford has done the near impossible: He's written, produced and sold two great sitcom pilots in one year. ABC's *The Drew Carey Show* and a blue-collar domestic comedy called *Bless This House* for CBS. Bruce asks Jane and me to run one show while he runs the other. Les Moonves, then president of Warner Bros., tells us to take *Bless This House* because "*Drew Carey* won't last six weeks."

* * *

Jane is leery of working with Andrew. She's a woman. And women hate Andrew "Dice" Clay. That is, until they see him with his son, whom he adores, and realize "The Diceman" is an act.

Andy is a nice Jewish boy from Brooklyn who feeds his family by saying despicably vile things to women in a broad Italian-New Yawk accent.

* * *

"So, I've got my tongue up this broad's ass … in line at the bank, when…"

* * *

We met Andrew a few months earlier when we worked on a six-episode Ralph Macchio series that never made it to air. Andrew, whose career was at a low point at the time, tried reinventing himself by taking a small role as Ralph's cousin and billing himself as "Andrew Clay," hoping that dropping "Dice" would fool the millions of TV-watching women he'd offended throughout his career.

He was fantastic. His comic timing impeccable. Everyone walked away from that series thinking they'd starred the wrong guy — including the women who hadn't wanted him on the show in the first place. Within weeks, the Macchio show was dead, and Andrew had his own CBS deal.

* * *

Andrew is rarely "off."

"You're married to Adrienne Barbeau? You are so lucky. I would throw my wife off a cliff for her."

* * *

"Milmore, when I'm done with you, you'll be bowlegged for life."

* * *

Andrew always calls Jane "Milmore." I'm "Van Zandt." And Bruce Helford is "The Bug" (but only behind his back, as in "Where the hell is the Bug?") because he's always buzzing in his ear. Andrew, always with "Hot Tub Johnny" or "Club Soda Kenny" at his side, carries hundred-dollar bills in a big roll, so he can peel them off to make one of his assistants run to McDonald's or spontaneously buy new car tires for a crew member.

* * *

Cathy Moriarty stars as his wife. She's a doll. A foul-mouthed doll, but a doll nonetheless.

We meet Cathy at a classy ladies-who-lunch bistro on Sunset Plaza Drive. The three of us, and a restaurant filled with Nancy Reagan types. Cathy and Jane hit it off immediately. Two loud, fun, outspoken East Coast girls. A little too outspoken. Every other word from Cathy is "fuck." And loud.

"I was with this one fuckin' guy who broke my fuckin' back when he threw me across the fuckin' room."

All the Nancy Reagans stop talking.

"What are you lookin' at?"

The Nancy Reagans look away.

"Want to see the scar?"

"No, that's OK."

Cathy rises and starts to pull up her shirt to show the scar anyway.

"Check, please."

* * *

Andrew and Cathy are a great team.

They've been friends forever. I can't tell if they dated in the old days or not. There's definitely a history there, and together the chemistry is perfect. They're loving, funny and touching. As real a married couple as you'll see on television.

And off-screen, Cathy has no trouble telling Andrew to shut up, fuck off, or, "Learn your goddamn lines."

This could make my job easy.

* * *

Being executive producer on someone else's show is a bit thankless. You run the show, making all the minute-by-minute decisions but ultimately defer to the creator of the show whenever he or she shows up. In our case, Bruce Helford runs *The Drew Carey Show* full-time in a nearby set of offices, and he joins us before or after his Drew workday a couple of days a week.

Bruce is unlike anyone I've ever worked with. He's a master at producing hit shows. He has a brilliant feel for what works and what doesn't. He has endless rules for why TV shows are hits and others are not. He's a great writer. And he works like a dog, examining every speck of every script.

We work so differently — which might explain why he has 4,000 shows on the air and I do not. I think you should be able to get your job done from 9-to-5. Bruce thinks that if you aren't there all night, every night, sweating blood, you aren't working hard enough.

His solution is to make the one rewrite night he's with us each week more "fun" by going for "comedy walks" at 3 a.m. These are walks that take us around the studio lot, designed to get you out of the room and freshen your mind.

Walk down Western Street where Eastwood filmed *Unforgiven*. Trek across *McHale's Navy's* dried-up lagoon. Climb the stairs back to the Writers' Room. These walks do nothing but make me even more tired, and 15 minutes later to go home than if we hadn't walked anywhere.

* * *

I give Bruce a hard time about his hours. But he can't help it — that's the way he works. He pontificates the minutest of details for hours — as the writing staff watches dinner plans they'd made with their wives disappear and excuse themselves to give away season tickets for Lakers games.

One night, *The Simpsons* co-creator Sam Simon, who consults for us two days a week, draws a clock on the wall behind Bruce's back and keeps re-drawing the minute hand to show how much time Bruce is spending dissecting a line.

* * *

Five episodes in, and the show is going like clockwork. Then Rosie O'Donnell is brought on to play Andrew's sister.

The week goes well until the first run-through, when Rosie makes her entrance and the audience of studio execs applauds.

Afterward, we get a note from Andrew.

"I want an entrance."

"But the scene starts with you on stage washing dishes."

"Rosie gets an entrance. I want an entrance, too."

"Andrew, it makes no sense for you to have an entrance. You're already onstage washing dishes at the top of the scene."

"How are people supposed to clap for me if I'm already there?"

The compromise: Andrew has his back to the audience as he washes the dishes, and turns around on the word "Action" so the audience can applaud him as he rinses the pots when they see his face for the first time.

Only two people applaud. "Hot Tub Johnny" and "Club Soda Kenny."

* * *

"Billy, Rosie O'Donnell's on the phone."

"Hi, Rosie. What's up?"

"I'm on the set, and I'm looking at this script, and I have some notes for you."

Jane laughs at me from her desk, knowing I'm too nice to tell our hired-gun guest-star to go screw herself.

"What seems to be the problem? The episode is great this week."

"I'm not talking about this episode. This is the one where Cathy goes looking for houses."

"That's next week's script."

"Right."

"You have notes on next week's script?"

"Yes."

"But you're not in that script."

A pause, then Rosie says, "So?"

I pause, then say, "OK, Jane will be right down to the set to take your notes."

* * *

One night after a long rewrite with Bruce in the room with us, we reach a scene that takes place in a car. Bruce tells us why he doesn't like blue-screen car scenes, but how it costs $10,000 more to use a regular car outdoors.

Sam Simon begs, "I'll pay you the ten thousand dollars. Just turn the goddamn page!"

* * *

Cathy's started to gain a little weight. It happens on every show. With a caterer and a table of junk food sitting behind the set all day, every day, how could it not? Plus, Cathy's own restaurant, Mulberry Street, caters great Italian food for us backstage every night we shoot the show.

We don't care that she's gaining weight. At all. But Cathy says she's working out with a trainer. When the costumer brings her clothes to try on, Cathy refuses to wear them. She says they're the wrong size.

But they're not the wrong size. They're the size that will fit her.

Without Cathy's knowledge, the costumer takes out the labels and sews in labels one size smaller. Cathy says, "That's more like it," and agrees to try the clothes on. And she continues to unknowingly wear the one-size-larger clothes for the rest of the series, all the while talking about how much weight she keeps losing.

* * *

Sam Simon walks into the Writers' Room, unaware we've been sitting here for two hours beating our heads against the wall trying to come up with a new storyline.

He says, "Hey, on my way over here I had an idea for a show."

In literally five minutes he tells us a spectacular story, breaks down the structure of each scene, and pitches so many usable jokes that with another hour's worth of work, anyone in the room can finish writing the script.

Then he sits down.

"What are we working on?"

* * *

Every Thursday, we get a call from the director to come to the set.

"Andrew keeps pretending there's a fly buzzing around his head in the scene and won't stop."

"Andrew wants to say the word 'bop' after each line. He says it'll be his new catchphrase."

"Andrew refuses to wear his postal uniform without rolling the sleeves up like a biker."

"Andrew wants to smoke in this scene."

"Andrew keeps talking in a Spanish accent."

It takes us four or five shows to realize Thursday is simply the day Andrew is supposed to have his script memorized. And stalling all day with inane problems gives him more time to learn his lines.

* * *

Elaine Stritch comes to town.

One of Broadway's greatest actresses, with a reputation as a pain in the ass. I've never worked with her and don't care what the reports are.

She's brilliant, and I'm honored to have her come play Cathy's mother in the Christmas episode. We realize we're in trouble when the driver picks her up and says, "Good morning," and she answers, "There'll be none of that!"

They drive in silence.

Arriving at the studio, he shows Miss Stritch to her dressing room. She walks in, looks around, and screams.

"What is that couch doing in here? Do you think I'm here to fucking entertain people? Get it out! Out!"

* * *

I arrive for the table-read and can't find our production assistant. "Where's Larry Rickles?"

"He went across the street to get Miss Stritch coffee."

"We have coffee right here."

"It didn't smell good enough for her."

Everyone from the studio comes to the table reading of this script. It's one of the best ones we've done, and everyone's excited that Andrew is going to do his Elvis impression singing "Blue Christmas" when his practically broke character gives it as a Christmas gift to his wife.

On this day, Bruce Helford is there to run things. He rises to welcome our very special guest this week, Miss Elaine Stritch. Everyone applauds.

Elaine rises. "Do you want me to read the lines I rewrote in my hotel last night, or do you want me to just read this shit?"

Bruce answers, "Please just read our shit."

* * *

Later in the week, Jane and I are called to the set. Elaine is sobbing, and no one can figure out what's wrong. They've been sitting there for 15 minutes.

Jane takes over: "I'll handle it. This is like dealing with my mother."

She brusquely turns to Elaine. "What's the problem, Elaine?"

Finally, she blurts it out: "My character would never refer to her daughter's rear end as a 'can'!"

"She's not. You're quoting Andrew's character."

"Oh."

Long pause.

"Well, then, that's different."

* * *

I notice Andrew sitting obediently, waiting to rehearse.

"Andrew, I can't help but notice you know all your lines and you're incredibly well-behaved this week."

He motions to Stritch. "Hey. There's only room for one."

* * *

It's the best show we do all season.

Elaine checks out of her hotel on the weekend and calls me at home to say they won't let her leave without paying the incidental bills she's racked up. Warner Bros. will only pay for the room itself. I get stuck paying $800 so she can make her plane.

Warner Bros. refuses to reimburse me.

* * *

The following week, on Thursday, comedy savant Andrew Clay decides he's going to say, "It's a touchy situation, Alice." In every episode. To create a new catchphrase. As in, "Whatchu talkin' 'bout, Willis?" and, "Kiss my grits."

"It's a touchy situation, Alice."

We beg him not to, but as we film a scene in front of the studio audience, out it comes:

"It's a touchy situation, Alice."

The problem is that it seems apparent he has no idea what the phrase means and keeps ad-libbing it where it makes absolutely no

144

sense. The next day, no one's repeating it around the country. That doesn't keep him from trying to use it the following week.

* * *

Sam Simon announces that I run the best room since the Charles Brothers on *Cheers*. That's like having Fred Astaire tell you you're a pretty good dancer.

* * *

On set, Jane leans over a table talking to the director. Andrew makes lewd comments about her backside.

Jane: "You know I could sue you for sexual harassment."

Andrew: "But you won't. I'll buy you a Mercedes to keep you happy."

Jane: "You're an asshole."

* * *

Cathy has had it with Andrew, too.

"I have a way to get him to learn his fucking lines. We won't pay him each week until he can prove he's memorized the script."

* * *

Against the wishes of all the "Dice"-haters in the country, the show is picked up for the back nine episodes. I'm proud of this show. It handles middle-class life in a realistic way; the characters are all three-dimensional; the relationship between Andrew and Cathy is loving, funny, and honest; and the actors are all great — even the kids. They're not typical cutesy kid actors; they're good actors.

And the writing is stellar. A terrific staff of the town's best writers. We get to explore real teenage issues, as well as real marital issues, money issues, friendship issues. None of the storylines is sewn up each week like a corny sitcom. We have arcs for each character that run for the entire season. To me it's as good a show as *Roseanne*.

(That's another Bruce Helford show, by the way — his hours may aggravate me, but he's incredibly gifted.)

Even the ratings are solid.

CBS and Warner Bros. are happy enough to renegotiate a huge deal with Jane and me. (When it's all but settled, I make them add another Elaine Stritch-worth $800 on top.) Rosie O'Donnell is hired for two more episodes. And Les Moonves, the man who shepherded the show as president of Warner Bros. Studio has been promoted to president of CBS — the network that airs the show. Looks like we're going to be here for a nice, long run.

* * *

Two episodes later — 11 a.m.

The CBS executive covering our show gives us notes after a Monday morning read-through of what could be our best script to date.

Bruce Helford gets a phone call in the greenroom in the middle of the session. He listens, asks if he can call back, and hangs up. The note session continues. The CBS executive leaves.

The door closes.

Bruce turns to Jane and me.

"We just got canceled."

"What?!"

"That phone call I got? From Warner Bros. They just got the call from CBS."

"CBS was here."

"Apparently our CBS guy didn't know this was coming."

"The last time a show got ratings this high in our time slot was *Good Times* in the 1970s."

"They just picked us up, for God's sake! What happened?"

"No one knows. Les Moonves called Warner Bros. It's over."

* * *

We gather the actors and the crew, including our new director who was literally one hour into his first week with us, and we break the news. The kids start bawling. This is hard enough as an adult, but for a kid, this is cruel.

Andrew and Cathy hug everybody. Everyone wanders around in a daze. People are unsure whether they should go home, pack their dressing rooms up, or wait to see if this is a bad April Fools' joke and they'll have to go back to work.

Bruce Helford returns to the *Drew Carey* offices. Jane and I return to our "development" office to create a new show of our own. On my way I pass through the lobby of the Warner Bros. casting office. There, seated with script pages in his hands waiting to audition for a new show, is Don Stark — the third lead from our show. Literally 30 minutes after the show got canned. He motions to the script pages in his hand.

"Hey, I gotta work."

* * *

I get a call that night. Apparently before he left, Andrew and "Hot Tub Johnny" stuffed props and furniture and costumes from the set into Andrew's truck and drove off the lot.

I see what's left of the set the next day. I think Andrew even took the nails out of the walls.

* * *

Cathy goes back to her movie career and "Mulberry Street," her incredible restaurant in Beverly Hills. (Get the eggplant parmigiana and the white cake.)

* * *

No one ever gave us the official reason for being canceled. Rumor has it somebody's wife at General Electric didn't want Andrew on her husband's network, and that was that.

* * *

Andrew mistakenly thinks we got canceled because he alienated his "Dice" fans. He tells people that if only we'd let him play the "Dice" character that all of America loves we'd have been a smash hit. He decides to go back out on tour. To out-Dice "The Diceman" and give people what they really want.

* * *

Seven years later, I open *TV Guide* fearfully looking for either *The Wayans Bros.* or *Daddy Dearest* to be named on their list of the "Fifty Worst Television Shows of All Time." They're not on the list.

But No. 48: *Bless This House.*

Some people won't be happy until Andrew is hanged in the town square like Mussolini.

It's a touchy situation, Alice.

A WIN-WIN SITUATION

Brooke Shields and "Suddenly Susan"

Brooke Shields is offered her own TV show after guest starring on *Friends*, where she licked Matthew Perry's hands for laughs. Nobody licks funnier than Brooke, I guess.

The project she chooses to star in is called *Suddenly Susan,* a one-camera dramedy, which is a TV term for a humorous drama — or as I like to think of them, comedies that aren't funny.

It's about a character that has gone from her parents' home straight into a serious relationship; at the start of the pilot she breaks up with her fiancé, suddenly left to face life on her own. Not so-and-so's daughter. Not so-and-so's fiancée. She's suddenly just Susan.

NBC has given the project the OK but decided the series has to be rewritten as a three-camera sitcom to fit in with *Friends* and *Seinfeld* and all its other "Must-See TV" shows.

Clyde Phillips, the author of the piece (a brilliant writer known for *Parker Lewis Can't Lose* and eventually *Dexter* and *Nurse Jackie*, among many others), has been given the assignment of switching his one-camera script (written like a movie) into a multi-cam format (performed live in front of an audience and filmed with multiple cameras all shooting at once).

When we eventually meet him, he instantly endears himself to me by saying how hard it is to do what we do. Or rather — in his words —

he has to "stop thinking intelligently" and "get down into the sewer with a funny hat on" to write this 'shit.'" Cute.

We come into the picture when the people at Warner Bros. read his "shit" and, let's just say, aren't happy with the job he's done. Warner Bros., the biggest supplier of product in the television business (and the company paying for this series), decides not to show the script to Brooke for fear she'll back out of the project. If the show is not cast, filmed, and edited within two weeks, there will be no series.

Two weeks to get any show up and running is, quite simply, insane. Most TV shows get eight weeks at the start of each season — and that's after a finished pilot has been created and worked on, written, cast, shot, and edited the year before.

Jane and I refuse the offer. We've never worked for NBC. We know no one over there, and no one there knows us. There are only four major networks at this time, so we only get four chances to impress or fail. The time constraints are ridiculous, and rumor has it the script should be thrown out. Taking this job doesn't seem like the smartest way to start a relationship with a network.

Besides, we're starting rehearsals for our play *Confessions of a Dirty Blonde* back East in 12 days. (A play written in plenty of time, by the way!) My rehearsal schedule can't be changed, and the show is already sold out. We say, "No, thank you."

David Janollari calls to ask if we could at least read the script and give NBC notes. We could certainly do that. The studio is paying us a huge salary to "develop." They aren't paying us to go do a play. We say yes. Jane reads the script at her desk, which sits opposite mine. For an hour neither one of us says anything.

Finally, Jane looks up and says, "This stinks."

We call Warner Bros. to say we pass. David asks, "So what do you think?"

Jane says, "I think you should cancel the entire project, traipse Brooke Shields out at the NBC announcements in NYC in two weeks, when they announce their fall schedule, say you're developing a new show for her, get everybody all excited to see her, and then give us six weeks to come up with a decent premise."

David says that isn't possible. This has to happen right now. "Don't you think you could pull it off? You did *The Wayans Bros.* with a lot less talent. And they're looking for this to go between *Friends* and *Seinfeld*."

I say, "I'm sorry, but we start rehearsals for a play back East in two weeks. We wouldn't have the time to do this even if we wanted to."

He talks us into sitting in on a casting session for the grandmother role that is taking place downstairs in our building. "It's one thing to read it. But once you see how funny it plays, you'll change your minds."

We go downstairs and see a roster of legendary talents: Nancy Marchand, Elizabeth Ashley, Carol Channing, Glynis Johns, and Gretchen Wyler, among others, all reading for the role. It still isn't funny to us.

Again, we say, "No, thank you."

David asks, "Well, what would you do to fix it if you could?"

Off the top of our heads Jane and I volunteer one general note after another. Let the humor come from the characters. Make the characters real people. If the jokes don't advance the story, they don't belong in the script. Lose the French chef with the funny accent and the funny hat. Basic stuff.

David thinks and says: "OK. I understand you don't want to do the job, but would you at least meet with NBC and give them these notes? It could save us."

* * *

Jane and I walk into Hampton's, a lunch place known for serving hamburgers 64 ways, near the Burbank studios. Sitting at a back table is not only Warren Littlefield, the president of NBC, but 20 other people sitting around him looking up at us with notepads.

Jane and I have no idea what to make of this.

And what is Clyde Phillips doing here? We thought they'd fired him. How on earth are we supposed to give these extensive notes on this guy's script if he's sitting right there? He's a talented, successful guy — this is going to be awkward, to say the least.

Warren Littlefield stands and says, "On behalf of NBC I'd like to thank Billy and Jane for coming aboard and taking over *Suddenly Susan.*"

What?!

Everybody applauds, except for us — and Clyde Phillips, who, it appears, is hearing this news for the first time along with us. We're trapped. We look over at David Janollari, who is giggling into his hands. We realize we've been suckered. (Jane swears to this day she almost reached for the silverware bowl in the middle of the table to grab a knife to stab him with.)

Warren Littlefield asks for our notes. Clyde's prematurely bald head starts to turn beet-red. Warren waves a hand in front of Clyde's face without looking at him and says, "And don't worry about pulling any punches, we all know the whole script, as is, is shit."

Yikes.

We start, trying to be as delicate as we can as we pick apart Clyde's work. At the end of our spiel, Warren says: "Perfect. That's exactly what I want. Start writing. We go to the table on Wednesday."

"No problem." I say. What have we gotten ourselves into?

But it's Thursday afternoon. We'll need a script done by Monday to give the other departments working on the show time to do their jobs for a Wednesday table-read.

Where do we begin? Who is this Susan character? What is the voice of the show? What's the theme of the show? What does Susan do for a living? Who are the other characters? Where does this take place? Did they say they had sets built already? Why is Jane shooting David Janollari those looks and staring at those knives?

I'm relieved as I realize we're covered technically. Emmy-winner Barnett Kellman is already set to direct, with credits that include *Murphy Brown, Something Wilder,* and *Mad About You.* Our good friend Frank Pace is producing, so I know all our usual great crew and camera people are going to be in place.

Everyone gets up to leave, except for Jane and me.

I stop the exodus to ask Warren to address the casting problem. By the time we finish the script there will be no time left to see actors audition. Recalling who we saw reading the day before, we ask to cast the brilliant Nancy Marchand as the grandmother and Elizabeth Ashley as Brooke's boss. Warren says fine.

He also agrees to let us cast David Krumholz (the comedic kid from *Staten Island 10309*) as the office nebbish. We're told by Warren that Maggie Wheeler, who was funny on *Friends* in a recurring role, should play Brooke's wisecracking best friend.

Great. We have half the actors cast. For a show that doesn't exist.

David Janollari ends the meeting with the words he's famous for saying to writers right before he walks out of a Writers' Room and leaves you on your own to make sense of the mess he's laid at your feet. "Let's do it!"

* * *

We meet with Brooke that night at a secret dinner meeting set up by Warner Bros. Our agent tells us Clyde isn't there because has been fired from this project — except for the minor detail that no one actually fired him. He'll be in the room with us all week long, and we should "just ignore him."

Brooke meets us at a restaurant in the Valley, and she couldn't be sweeter. We all admit the circumstances of working together are unusual, and truly how bad we all feel about what's happening to Clyde, and how awkward this is. Brooke's agent speaks for the first time.

"He'll feel better when the show's on the air for five years and he gets a big check."

The one thing we don't tell Brooke is that the only reason we're here is because we were tricked into this and have no way out without alienating one of the four major network heads.

The clock is ticking, and we still have no idea what we're doing. Jane and I are about to tell Brooke that we came up with a backdrop for the series that everybody likes and Warren has approved. "Susan" will work in the fashion world at a magazine like *Vogue* or *Cosmopolitan*. We figure that by using the fashion world, we can play on who Brooke is, as well as her beauty, and get some good stories from her own life while we're at it.

I start. "Jane and I gave this a lot of thought, and we definitely want to lose the Denny's test kitchen thing from Clyde's script."

Brooke says, "Good."

So far, so good.

"I'm really open to anything."

Great!

"There's just one thing."

Jane and I share a look.

"Whatever we do, I just … don't feel comfortable … playing myself or having any premise involving the fashion world."

"Good." I answer. "Because … we were thinking of something entirely different than that."

By the end of the night, the three of us settle on having Susan work at a publishing firm as a novice editor, having to edit for a larger-than-life Barbara Cartland-like romance novelist — to be played by the already-cast Elizabeth Ashley. We'll write her a different role.

When we part, our heads still spinning, Jane and I race back to the lot to look at the sets Clyde had built to be part of his restaurant show and then figure out how to change them from a Denny's headquarters test kitchen into a book publisher's office without spending any more money — for scenes that we haven't even written yet.

The other problem with the sets, we realize, is they were built *deep*, as though we're filming a one-camera show — the way a movie set is built so you can take a camera way into the set and film a million different angles. An incredibly deep set for a sitcom is a waste of space. A sitcom is acted like a play, and the cameras sit out front and shoot straight ahead. That's why you'll notice the rooms in the background of a sitcom set are never used.

As we try to move walls around, we realize the best entrance on the existing set is out of the audience's view. Not only do we have sets that make no sense for what we're about to do, they aren't functional either.

Back at the office, we put on sweats, open a "good luck" basket from NBC filled with Jolt Cola and everything made out of sugar and caffeine they could cram into the basket, set out the M&Ms and the tub of Red Vines, and start to barrel through the script. We pilfer a library of our unfinished projects looking for snatches of romantic comedy dialogue to rip off for Susan and her soon-to-be-ex-boyfriend for the opening scene.

There's *nothing*. We'll have to create this from scratch.

Keeping the same basic structure from the original script, we divide scenes up and start writing. Luckily I don't believe in writer's block. For me, get something down on paper and fix it later. It's always easier to rewrite than write.

I hate everything Jane writes on her pink legal pads in her girly longhand and spend most of the next hour making fun of her spelling. She reads the scenes I write as quickly as the printer spits them out and tells me they're too mean-spirited and overwritten.

"Yeah? Try spelling 'banana!'"

"Shut up! And you have three jokes every place you only need one!"

I tell her, "Yeah but with all the extra jokes, I just nailed 10 pages out of a 42-page script."

By 3 a.m., we find an opening to the show we think works and immediately start to calm down, catch our breaths, and start over — writing for real. Together.

We write a scene, print it out, read it. Not good enough.

Jane cries. I crumple script pages and curse.

More sugar. And I start on my sixth Coca-Cola. (No Jolt for me)

We start over.

By 5 in the morning it starts to resemble a script.

And we're sick to our stomachs from all the junk we ate.

That's when Clyde starts to call every hour to ask, "How's it going?"

In the middle of the next day, I look up from the computer to find Jane is nowhere to be seen. I assume she's pretended to go for a walk so she could sneak off and take a nap somewhere leaving me to do all the work, so I start walking down the hall looking for her so I can yell at her instead of writing.

Through an open door in his office I see David Janollari, his hands on his hips, gyrating, as Jane looks on, completely embarrassed.

It seems Warren Littlefield has called David, sure some new song is going to sweep the nation and we should get a jump on everyone by including it in our script. The only thing funnier than Jane's mouth hanging open is David singing the song a cappella and acting it out in his office with the door wide open.

The song Warren Littlefield wants in the script before it sweeps the nation? "La Macarena."

* * *

The table-read Wednesday morning: The actors sit at a long conference table on the soundstage, with the writers and director at the head. In director chairs off to either side sit the studio and network people. Since this is an "important project," there are what seems like 50 more network and studio people sitting up in the bleachers, where the audience for live TV shows usually sits.

Jane and I stagger in, hopeful we've pulled this off. We created a show from scratch in four days.

We hope.

Everything rides on whether Warren Littlefield finds this funny.

I welcome everyone and introduce the actors. Director Barnet Kellman opens the script and reads the title.

I see Warren Littlefield's people are already scribbling notes in the margins of the script — and we haven't even begun.

The reading begins. I have to hold my breath only until the first line. David Krumholz opens his mouth and is so perfectly funny that the ice is broken. He gets such huge laughs it even drowns out Janollari's fake laugh "Ha HAA!"

From here forward the script is one home run laugh after another, right to the end.

Elizabeth Ashley had arrived at the studio thinking she was playing a boss-from-hell, was handed her script and, after I told her what was going on, immediately adjusted with an "OK … " to instantly become a Southern Belle romance novelist.

Nancy Marchand is hilarious as the grandmother. Krumholz is hilarious. Phil Casnoff as the boss is hilarious. Maggie Wheeler is hilarious. And, thank God, Brooke is hilarious — without having to lick Matthew Perry's hands.

The reading ends. Everyone applauds. Jane and I collapse. The actors are told to go to lunch for an hour, so the network can give us notes. Elizabeth Ashley gives us a "Thank you, Sugar Britches" in her best Tallulah Bankhead voice, as Jane, Clyde, and I move to the living-room set, where Warren Littlefield and an exec I never met before start to give us notes and ask for changes.

"In the first scene, I don't think Brooke's character would do that," says the exec I just met and immediately don't like.

I think; "Is that right? How would you know? And by the way, *who* are you?"

I guess I was still expecting pats on the back and kudos. Didn't anyone remember we pulled this all together in four days? They give us notes like we've been working on this for a year.

Most of Warren's notes start with the words, "On *Caroline in the City,* we found it best when…" Evidently he feels responsible for the success of *Caroline in the City* — a pet project of his from the past — and plans on turning this into another *Caroline in the City*. There's one problem: I didn't care for *Caroline in the City*.

I write down everything Warren says. (Jane takes pride in memorizing everything without the need to ever write down notes or even carry a script for reference.) I tell him we'll take care of it all, knowing we'll fix whatever we were going to fix anyway. As we leave the soundstage, Clyde discusses the notes with Jane.

"That doesn't sound so bad at all. So, what? We do one scene tonight and another scene tomorrow? And by shoot day we'll be in great shape, right?" Jane explains to Clyde that this isn't done like a one-camera show. We have to rewrite every single scene tonight, and that tomorrow there will be another run-through, where we'll get more notes and do this all again—and so on, all week long.

I'm 10 feet away, but I see every ounce of blood drain out of his face.

We enter the Writers' Room to find 15 of our funniest writer friends sitting there, waiting to help with the rewrite. The only one I don't know is Bob Ellison, a legendary punch-up guy whose hand has been in practically every good TV comedy for the last 20 years. Sent over by NBC.

Luckily it turns out we didn't have a lot of writing to do. Everything worked.

When we get to one spot that does need a tweak, Clyde starts pitching something from his original script. That's sort of a no-no in the Writers' Room. If something gets changed from a first-draft script, there's usually a reason.

After Clyde pitches his original joke again, Bob Ellison tells him what you tell every novice writer who invariably does the same thing: "Why don't you save that joke and put it in your pilot?"

Then Bob catches himself. "Oh, that's right. This is your pilot."

* * *

Show night. Nine days since we were sitting in Hampton's, getting railroaded into taking the job. We're dead on our feet. All I know for sure at this point is that Brooke without makeup is the most beautiful woman you'll ever meet. And Brooke *with* makeup — wow.

Before every pilot shoot I give the actors a pep talk, to thank them, relax them, pump them up, and give it a real opening night feel. We gather all the actors together behind the set. I give my "win one for the Gipper"-like speech. Everyone's pumped up. Brooke seems confident.

Barnet Kellman steps in. And with all the pep of a minister burying the dead, he says: "Don't get nervous if the audience doesn't think you're funny. We can always do another take. Even if the audience has to leave and we have to stay here all night."

On that note, our actors take their places.

It goes surprisingly well. Until a scene where Brooke tries to loosen up by smoking cigars and doing Jell-O shots in a bar, where she gets incredibly drunk. The scene bombs. So they do it again. And again. The audience goes from laughing to chuckling to silence. All I can hear is the pounding of my heart and David Janollari's fake laugh "Ha HAA!" which has taken on a desperate tone.

A halt is called in the shooting. Warren Littlefield, his people, the Warner Bros. people, Jane and me — and, of course, Clyde — meet around the kitchen table set with the actors and audience looking on. It's decided that we will shut down for the night — unheard of for a pilot. The audience is sent home, and Jane and I are instructed to rewrite the bar scene, which obviously didn't work, and we will re-shoot it tomorrow evening without an audience.

That night Jane, writer Matt Ember, and I rewrite the bar scene. Matt keeps bringing up the fact that the bar set was off to the side and the audience didn't react to it perhaps because they literally couldn't see it. As true as it may be, it isn't helpful.

The next day, two scenes to film. A three-page scene in a bedroom and the five-page scene in a bar. Stage them, camera-block them, and shoot them.

It's 9 a.m. How long can it take?

At 7 p.m., when I finally walk out to catch my red-eye flight, we are only halfway through camera-blocking the bar scene. Frank Pace takes over, and Jane and I leave. Should we have stayed in L.A.? Absolutely. But I don't think it would have changed a thing.

Jane and I go directly from Kennedy Airport at 5 a.m. to the theater, where we begin work on our play. And for the next three days, via the phone and Federal Express, we edit the show with Frank Pace and the editor in Los Angeles, and Jane and me on the East Coast.

We meet our Friday deadline. Two weeks to the day when Warren Littlefield welcomed us "on board," we've created a show, wrote it, cast it, rehearsed it, filmed it, edited it and turned it in — and it's good.

* * *

One week later, Warren Littlefield steps out on the stage at New York's Lincoln Center in front of the NBC advertisers, executives, and journalists to announce the fall lineup. Following *Seinfeld* in the coveted spot at 8:30 Thursday nights? *Suddenly Susan.* The crowd goes crazy. Brooke walks out onto the stage. They go even crazier.

I hear this from friends, because we aren't there. No one bothers to call us to give us the good news, let alone invite us.

That night NBC holds a big celebratory party in New York. Jane and I go, assuming our not being invited was an oversight, along with the good news phone call. Every person we see there — and we know almost everyone by now — has a slight hesitation on his or her face, fol-lowed by: "Congratulations!"

* * *

The next morning, Jane meets me at my New Jersey house. So many thoughts are filling my head. "We have to get a writing staff to-gether before other shows get the writers we want. How soon can we start? Where will the offices be? We want to sit with Brooke and discuss the process and everything we want to change. We want to hire specific directors before they get booked. Why isn't anyone, including my agent, calling me back?" Jane's main thought is: "What the hell is epi-sode No. 2 going to be?"

The phone rings. It's our manager.

"They … decided to replace you."

"Who?"

"NBC. You've been fired from *Suddenly Susan*."

"What?! Why?"

"Warren didn't connect with you."

"What does that mean?"

"I have no idea."

* * *

Maybe Warren had other people in mind before we were even asked and they were unavailable at the time — or smart enough to say no. Maybe it had something to do with me walking around on the soundstage with my plane ticket to JFK sticking out of my pocket and leaving before the re-shoots were finished.

Wasn't this supposed to be a "win-win" proposition? Turned out to be a "lose-lose." No one would hire us to run another show for a year.

We keep watching the pilot tape that first week trying to figure out what we did wrong. We have no idea.

We get to hear NBC tell the press they have to retool the pilot be-cause ours was so weak. And since no one ever gets to see it, we can't prove anyone wrong for saying so. Clyde was quoted as being thrilled about the change because Jane and I "had no souls."

Murphy Brown writers Steve Peterman and Gary Dontzig are hired to replace us. We can't figure out why. Perfectly good writers, but why them and not us? And they get an entire six weeks to retool the thing, which is what we asked for in the first place.

Sometime that week, Steve Peterman calls to ask if I mind if he takes the job. I tell him of course not, thank him for calling, and wish them luck. I tell Jane how decent it is that Steve called. She points out he already had the job when he called to ask permission to take the job. I don't care; it's the thought that counts.

By the time Steve and Gary are done "retooling," Brooke is back working for a magazine. What bugs me is they replace every single brilliant actor we'd hired. I ask Warner Bros. why and am told, "They were good. They were too good." Whatever that means.

It's by sheer good luck the fabulous Nancy Marchand is let go. Were it not for NBC's cleaning house, she would not have been free to star in her career-defining role as Livia Soprano on *The Sopranos*.

* * *

As Steve and Gary film the second "Susan" pilot — which we did not attend, thank you very much — we find consolation knowing that at least we'll get our "developed by" credit on the show when it finally airs. Knowing that Clyde created the show, we've arranged contractually to receive a "Developed by Billy Van Zandt & Jane Milmore" credit, which would play over the opening show credits every week.

With all the press the show is getting, it looks like it could be a "win-win" situation after all. A win if it becomes a hit because we'll literally get part of the credit for it, and a win if it bombs because the industry will know we'd been released — and think perhaps if they'd kept us on it would have been a hit.

Over the next few weeks, on the sly, we continue to get calls from friends at the network who whisper how at NBC they refer to our version of the pilot as "the funny version." The only consolation I have is a weekly royalty check and knowing we own a percentage of the syndication rights — if they ever get to the requisite 100 episodes.

A few distant friends who haven't heard the news about our being fired send us good luck flowers the night the show premieres.

I couldn't be closer to the TV set. The writing credits for the pilot script are granted to all five of us — Clyde, Steve, Gary, Jane, and me. Barnett has done his usual great job. I'm glad to see Brooke is much more relaxed in this version, but funnier in ours — to my biased eye.

There is only one thing missing from the show: our names. The credits read, "Created by Clyde Phillips" as we expect. But following that comes the credit "Developed by Steve Peterman & Gary Dontzig."

And then — nothing. I keep thinking I blinked.

I call Frank Pace at home to ask what happened to our "developed by" credit — honestly thinking it is an oversight.

"You really ought to call Warner Bros."

We do. We're told: "Steve and Gary are the show runners, and we have to please them, so, too bad." Our agent screams that we have a contract and that without us they wouldn't even have a show on the air. The answer, from the studio we are still under contract to for another year: "So, sue us."

We don't. We do, however, call the Writers Guild, which immediately responds by telling us that while "created by" credits are covered by the Guild, "developed by" credits are not under Guild jurisdiction. Thanks, WGA. So, too bad indeed.

* * *

Technically we still haven't been fired by NBC. To this day no one has ever called us "officially" to say so. But then no one in the TV business gets fired. Instead, they act like they don't see you standing there until you get the hint.

* * *

After Jane and I are let go, I ask for just one thing. I want the photo of Brooke and me that we took together on the set the first day when they shot the cast PR pictures. I keep asking for it. The NBC publicity department says there is no such photo — it must not exist. And that is that.

* * *

I visit the *Suddenly Susan* set only once after we are let go. Tony Bennett is guest-starring. Frank Pace calls me over so I can meet Mr. Bennett and hear him sing. Brooke waves excitedly when she sees me on the set and comes over to give me a kiss and ask about my kids. I still love this girl.

* * *

Despite its insane beginning, *Suddenly Susan* lasts 100 episodes.

Do I feel that Jane and I are responsible in some small way for that? No. Steve, Gary, and Brooke are the reasons for that success. And Clyde. Without the original script, Brooke wouldn't have said yes and none of this would have happened.

I do, however, think we showcased Brooke well and helped sell her as a viable sitcom star. I also believe the series we had in mind would have been funnier. But who knows? Our version could have been funnier but still might have lasted for only one season. It's TV. There is no exact science. No matter what you do or how many times you test your show, they succeed when they're supposed to and fail the same way. And as Jane always says, "If testing TV shows actually worked, they'd all be hits."

I run into Brooke every now and then; she's always as sweet as the first day I met her. I wonder what she thinks of the whole experience. And I wonder if she'd ever work with us again.

And I still want that picture.

* * *

Epilogue:

Two years after *Suddenly Susan* is off the air, I come home one night to find this phone message. "Billy? Hi, this is Steve Peterman. Could you call me? It's about the audit."

Each of us who owns a piece of the show is auditing the Warner Bros. books so we can all be issued advance checks on our *Suddenly Susan* syndication deals. From the panicked sound of Steve's voice, I'm afraid he's spoken to the auditor and is about to tell me that Warner Bros. is claiming there is no profit to be shared. I hear the Warner Bros. president in my head: "So, sue us." I immediately call back. "What's wrong, Steve?"

He hems and haws and then he says, "I don't know how to ask you this, but I just got the report from the auditors and…"

Out it comes. He isn't calling to tell me Warner Bros. is robbing us. He only wants to know one thing.

"When we go into syndication, are … are you going to make more money off the show than we are?"

It turns out that our auditing fees have been pro-rated according to the percentages we all own of the show. Steve had received his copy of the official papers, which listed what we are each paying for the audit, and couldn't figure out why Jane and I are paying more than he and his partner. I tell Steve I have no idea what he and Gary are making. He presses again, volunteering the percentage he and Gary have in their contract.

"Are you making more than we are?"

"Um … I guess so. Yes."

"GODDAMMIT!!"

I have to pull the phone away from my ear.

"How much more?!"

"Steve, I…"

"HOW MUCH MORE?!"

"…A lot."

"GODDAMMIT!!"

He says he and Gary had to work three long, hard years for their money and asks how long we had to work for ours: "Six months?"

"Two weeks."

"GODDAMMIT!!"

My agent may not return my phone calls as fast as I like these days, but somehow I don't seem to mind.

* * *

Oh. And NBC did eventually send me that photo I'd asked for.

Only it's a picture of Brooke and Clyde.

EXPLORING THE YOUTHFUL FUN AT CBS

Penny Marshall, Olympia Dukakis, Richard Mulligan, and "Waiting for God"

Penny Marshall mumbled. No, I take that back. Marlon Brando mumbled. Penny Marshall made incomprehensible noises that sound like a nasal vacuum cleaner after the plug has been pulled out of the wall.

Known to my generation as the legendary star of *Laverne & Shirley*, Penny was not only one of the funniest women on television, she was one of the most successful female movie directors of all time.

It's the late '90s, and Penny's production company has secured the rights to a British sitcom classic *Waiting for God*, about the relationship between two people who meet in a nursing home. Academy Award winner Olympia Dukakis has agreed to star in the series for American TV. And Penny and Olympia are interested in doing it with Jane and me.

Now we have to sell it to CBS.

We walk into historic Television City to pitch our show. In the third-floor lobby, I finally meet Penny Marshall.

"Penny, it's great to finally meet you in person."

"Geh...tooo..." she answers from inside a big cloud of cigarette smoke. I have no idea what she just said to me.

* * *

There are only two downsides to working with Penny Marshall: the constant cigarette smoke — thicker than what comes out of Jersey Turnpike oil refineries — and the fact that I couldn't understand a word she said. Penny had the energy of a teenager, a God-given ability of knowing what's funny and what's not, and a drugstore for a pocketbook. ("You need a Valium? It's in here somewhere." Or as she'd say it, "n-yeuh Valium? Is een eeh nyuh-wheuh.")

* * *

We follow Penny's red leather sneakers down the CBS Hall of Fame hallway, past huge black-and-white photos of all the classic CBS hits from the past — *I Love Lucy, The Honeymooners, All in the Family, Gunsmoke*. A star-studded anniversary photo with its historic stable of stars, including Lassie, Alfred Hitchcock, and my wife and her cast from *Maude*. Adrienne Barbeau from 20 years ago wishes me luck.

We arrive at a conference room, where about 50 people are crammed into office chairs. Why so crowded? Because the network president, Les Moonves, has decided to attend this pitch meeting personally.

Les enters the room. All his underlings smile up at him. He pretends he doesn't notice.

Inside the small, enclosed room, inside the no-smoking building, Jane and I begin to sell them *Waiting for God*. My eyes are watering from Penny's cigarette smoke as I lay out the premise of the show and the characters — with Jane jumping in with a joke or two to keep things light and keep me on track. Maybe only 30 scripts a year will get ordered by a network, and then only half of them will get filmed, so the pressure to score is on. I just hope it doesn't look like I'm crying.

Penny leaps in to talk about the series as well: "The goo thahh da proven…right dere…"

The room goes silent. She asks the room, "Know wha' I mea'?"

Everyone says, "Yes."

Every time she talks, Les looks over to his right to see if it's him or if I have any idea what Penny's saying. I smile. He smiles back. We all laugh at Penny when she pauses at the end of a sentence, assuming — correctly, we hope — that she has in fact made a joke. After a while the laughs are real, because she sounds insane.

It is a brief meeting. Les tells us how he loves the idea of the show, the star, Penny, and Jane and me as "two of his favorite writers." Then he tells us to start thinking of male leads, and thanks us for coming in.

Meeting's over. We walk Olympia out to the car where she speaks for the first time: "What the fuck just happened in there?"

I have no trouble understanding Olympia.

"We just sold the show."

"When? All I heard was a lot of nervous people laughing at small talk that wasn't very funny."

I assure her Les bought the show.

"Yeah? Well, that's great."

We walk a little further.

"Just tell me one more thing."

I say, "Sure. What is it?"

"Could you understand one fucking word Penny was saying? I thought I was going deaf."

* * *

Six weeks later, Jane and I give CBS a finished script. We sit in the same conference room at CBS to get our notes. This time, the meeting is with two other people, the "Comedy Development" people for CBS.

"We only have two notes from Les. In the scene on the boardwalk where the 'Tom' character opens up to Olympia's character, we need to see she's moved by the end of the speech."

That's an acting note. But I nod and say, "We'll look at that."

They go on: "Oh, and one more thing. And I want to be very clear about this. This is not my note. This is Les Moonves's note."

I brace myself for the worst.

"Can Olympia's character have been married once — like, 40 years ago or something? For like a week?"

Jane and I don't answer at first. We don't understand. Finally, I say, "Fine."

Back in the car Jane asks what the marriage note means. I tell her. "So people won't think she's a lesbian."

Back at our office, we give Olympia's character an ex-husband and make the change to the boardwalk scene. In the stage directions after Tom's big speech we write, "WE SEE SHE IS MOVED."

We send the script back to CBS. They call back immediately.

"Great rewrite."

We now get the official go-ahead to hire a director and find a cast.

* * *

Going off the "approved CBS director" list, we offer the show to a well-known man responsible for a long list of hit TV shows. He passes because, we're told, he hates the British series this is based on.

The second name on the list strings us along for about three weeks and then turns us down. He never had any intention of doing our show. He used the offer from our show to up his price on a second show that he *did* want to do. He's done this to us three years in a row now. Jane says, "We should get 10 percent."

The third director is interested but can't work out a scheduling conflict and passes.

Another prominent director is the next name on the CBS "approved list," and we're asked to consider him. Penny, Jane, and I all agree it's a great idea. And with Les Moonves's blessing, we agree to go with him.

When we call to set up an appointment his agent informs us, "Well, he'll have to read the script first."

"I thought he was interested."

"He is. In the idea of it."

I hang up the phone and send a script to the director Jane and I wanted in the first place, Andy Cadiff (*Spin City, Home Improvement* and, eventually, *Hot in Cleveland*) telling him he's our guy as soon as the last one turns us down.

The last one turns us down — with his agent telling us, "He never wanted to do it in the first place."

We hire Andy.

* * *

Before you can audition actors for a TV show, you have to go through a "network casting meeting." This is a meeting where you defend your vision of the series to people you've never met before. A master list of every "name" actor in town that's even potentially right for your show is drawn up to discuss your project. These meetings supposedly make your project not only good, but the greatest show of all time.

Waiting for God revolves around Diana Trent and Tom Ballard, two spirited residents of a retirement home who spend their time running rings around Harvey, the home's sleazy, oppressive manager.

Based on this preliminary casting meeting, we'll be on the air for 20 years. Everybody's there — including Les Moonves again. Everyone has opinions on who should play Tom, opposite Olympia — ranging from smart ("John Cleese") to stupid ("Is Red Skelton still alive?"), and a list is drawn up of "CBS-approved actors," including the order in which Jane and I may offer the role to the approved stars.

Inside the conference room, everyone starts to pare down the list.

Harvey Korman is crossed off the list as being "too sketchy."

Jason Robards for being "never funny."

Mel Brooks is taken off the list because "it'll turn into the Mel Brooks shtick show." (And this is bad why?)

Sid Caesar because "he looks like death."

Conrad Bain because he's "too well known" as Mr. Drummond from *Different Strokes*.

No one else is even considered.

The final approved list in order:

> Alan Alda,
>
> Leslie Nielsen,
>
> John Cleese,
>
> Peter Falk,
>
> Alan Arkin,
>
> Richard Mulligan,
>
> Donald Sutherland,
>
> Christopher Lloyd.

The truth is the first two names on the list are Jack Lemmon and Walter Matthau.

This is a time when legendary movie stars don't even consider doing TV. It's beneath them. But most of the people in the room actually think they'll consider doing our little sitcom.

None of the "approved" actors has any idea they're even being considered. It's a wish list. As the "suits" battle on with casting ideas, I think, "Gee, I hope Conrad Bain doesn't ask what I'm working on when Adrienne and I see him for dinner tomorrow night."

Olympia has her own ideas about casting when I call her back in New Jersey to fill her in on the approved names. She says: "Cleese is wrong. He's never been able to play empathy. But he is talented."

I mention Richard Mulligan's name (the man we're eager to end up with), and she's quick to answer: "I'm not doing a show with him. I wouldn't even want to do a staged reading with him. He's always acting, you're always aware of it. And those rubber faces... And he's bony. He's wrong because he's bony!"

I admit I don't follow what she's talking about.

"There's a sharpness about his features and about the person, and the character of Tom is not sharp."

She demands to know why people don't realize that Eli Wallach is perfect for the role. I tell her what Les said when I brought his name up: "Look at him. Whoever plays the role of Tom has to live five years, or no one makes a dime."

There's a slight pause. Then I hear: "Omigod. I'm learning so much about television."

* * *

Penny Marshall's Director of Comedy calls with Penny's reactions to the list: "Richard Mulligan is the favorite. And there's no way she'll have Peter Falk in this show."

* * *

As Alan Alda, Leslie Nielsen, and the others turn down offers to play Tom (and as Walter Matthau and Jack Lemmon continue to make motion pictures, unaware they're even part of our discussions), we start auditions for the supporting roles.

Penny is always out of the country or tied up in the dentist chair, so everything gets videotaped. All the meetings. All the casting sessions for the smaller roles. Her Director of Comedy sits in the back of every room with a video camera. Every evening Penny watches the videos either in whatever hotel room she's in or at home recuperating from her gum work, and she calls us the following morning to mumble her opinions as Jane and I stare at each other from across our desks and shrug because we can't understand a word she says.

* * *

We're told actors Chris Rich and Matt Frewer have apparently both "passed" on the role of "Harvey."

I didn't know we'd offered it to them.

I don't even know who Chris Rich is.

* * *

Penny calls from Paris in the middle of a set designer meeting. She saw the video of our auditioning semifinalist actors. She quickly goes through the list of names giving her opinion of each actor assuming I'm ready with a pen and a list of names, which I'm not.

"No…no…. no…medium…OK…OK…no…"

Ten seconds after we hang up, someone from her company calls to find out what his boss said. He tells us that "medium" is less than "OK" and better than "no."

* * *

CBS keeps sending over people for us to see in casting. A 400-pound man comes in for the role of social-climber ladies' man "Harvey." He can barely walk across the room. Then another obese guy walks in to read for the same role.

I look on the audition sheet and realize all these large guys are "CBS" suggestions, which tells me two things:

- CBS hasn't bothered to read the script or watch the British series we're basing this on, and

- CBS must think fat people are funny.

* * *

Jane and I have a meeting at the Four Seasons with Judge Reinhold (*Beverly Hills Cop*). Judge would make a terrific "Harvey." I recall the last time I saw him — at the final callback for *Fast Times at Ridgemont High*, where he and I were the two finalists for the role that ended up making his career. Part of me wonders what might have happened if I'd gotten that role instead of Judge. Part of me thinks things worked out fine, thank you. Besides, if we'd switched roles, I might have had to make that movie about the dancing cop, too.

After an hour, Judge informs us he can't play Harvey, because he's already booked to do another show, but it was nice to meet us. I pick up the check, and Jane shoots me a look that says, "Let *him* pay."

* * *

The studio casting session is where the people paying for the show get to put in their two cents. We narrow each role down to three finalists. We set each actor's deal in place so they can't negotiate a higher salary after they officially get the role. And once we get the studio approvals, we'll bring them across town to CBS, where Les Moonves and his people will ultimately choose our cast.

* * *

Into the studio session, which my writer friends always refer to as "The Nuremberg Trials."

Warner Bros. casting guru Barbara Miller is already mad over the number of people invited to sit in her office, setting a lovely tone for comedy as she bangs around chairs and moves her coffee table, muttering to herself.

Penny Marshall's smoking up the joint, and of course no one says not to because she's Penny Marshall. Barbara Miller lights up with her.

I crack a window.

And it begins.

A cool reception greets each actor, each of whom enters and reads with looks of terror while Penny and Barbara blow smoke in their faces.

I can't help but notice that only Penny, Jane, and I are laughing at the punchlines. The producers who sold Penny's company the rights to the series and Penny's people sit quietly, aware that Barbara Miller doesn't even want them here. Warner Bros.' president has folded arms. But at least he's smiling.

Some of the people in the room snicker through the readings, thinking no one can hear them. We find out later they were laughing about how ugly all the actors are.

Barbara Miller lets her ash drop. "Hey, if they looked good, they'd be in movies."

* * *

The star of a popular animated TV series reads for us but insists on rearranging the furniture first to suit her own staging of the scene. As she moves chairs and asks us to move our seating around, Penny clearly — and loudly — states, "We don't have time for her."

* * *

Penny gives another poor girl direction. "Thi tah...puh fahh nahhh." None of us can help the girl out, because we haven't got a clue what Penny said. The guy from Penny's company says, "Good note, Penny."

The actress smiles and nods at Penny with a look of terror.

She reads the scene again, making wildly different choices with her acting in the hopes that something she did was what Penny asked for.

As the actress leaves, Penny says "Guh...."

We think that means "good."

The door shuts behind her, and David Janollari has a "great idea." "The role of Harvey's mousy assistant 'Jane' should be played by someone sexy!"

Penny loudly whispers to me: "That little guy's an idiot."

I hear her clear as a bell.

And so does the little idiot.

The Warner president says, "He's right. CBS will be looking for attractive women. So we need to find 'cute ugly girls.'"

I ask what a cute ugly girl is.

He names a popular actress. "She's cute, but she's not va-voom. Which makes her cute ugly."

Jane doesn't know who the actress is, even though we've hired her three times in the past.

Penny mutters something that sounds like "Jesus Christ."

Someone says the woman mentioned is eight months pregnant. David raises his eyebrows and asks when she's going to deliver. As in, "Can we get her to induce early?" I pray he doesn't try, because he's so good at his job she'll probably say yes.

And so the first round of casting callbacks ends, with the Warner people cutting almost everyone from our list because "this isn't 'The Ugly Show,' you know."

Back to the drawing board.

* * *

Alan Arkin is interested in playing Tom. One of the funniest men in film. I can easily picture him and Olympia together. It's a good match. And it's Alan Arkin! It's well known at CBS that he's turned down 17 of its shows in the past. Everyone's excited that he's interested in ours.

Jane and I have breakfast with Mr. Arkin at the Peninsula Hotel, and we love the guy. He's charming, funny, intelligent, and perfect for this show.

As breakfast comes to a close, he says: "There's just one thing. I've had a specific way of working my entire career, and I can't go backwards now."

I ask which way he's talking about specifically.

"Improv." He says, "I always improv."

"Improv what?" I ask.

"The entire script," he says.

Jane chokes on her water.

"You mean like Robin Williams on 'Mork and Mindy'?"

"No."

"Here's the thing, Alan. This a sitcom," I say. "We have to lock in a script by Wednesday so the camera crew can be ready to shoot the show on Friday."

He understands, he says, but we have to understand that scripts are mere guidelines to him. However, he does love the character, the show, and our writing.

Jane asks, "You like our writing, but you won't say the words we wrote?"

He answers: "That's right."

I ask him, "Well, what exactly would you change in our script?"

He answers that he'll have to read it again and get back to us. "I never read it with the intention of actually saying the words out loud."

We relay our meeting to Olympia, who quickly closes the door on the possibility of playing straight man to Alan Arkin. She informs us she's not getting into bed "with a guy who's gonna get his rocks off while I just lay there."

* * *

Still without a leading man, Jane and I go to CBS with our final choices for all the supporting roles.

At the last minute, Warner has kicked one of our favorites for Harvey off the list because "he's not handsome enough."

That means it's either going to be Peter Scolari (*Newhart*) or Michael McKean (*This Is Spinal Tap, Laverne & Shirley*) for Harvey. Peter almost doesn't come. His agent plays hardball and refuses to drop Peter's asking price. Jane tells the agent that as much as we love Peter, we will not pay him more than we're paying the stars of our show.

The agent says that Peter has another pilot offer at Fox for twice what we're offering.

Jane says: "I read that show. If Peter would rather do that piece of shit than do our high-profile show with an Oscar-winning actress in a proven series, then that's his call. But maybe there's a reason Tom Hanks has a big film career and Peter's doing syndicated reality shows."

Peter's agent drops his price.

Jane's good at this.

* * *

I meet Peter in the CBS lobby and apologize to him for making him audition. He starred on *Newhart* for CBS for almost 10 years. One would assume they already know his work. He seems appreciative that I even care.

Michael McKean's quiet. I like that in a comedian.

Along with the other actresses reading for the role of "Jane," Harvey's whipping-dog assistant, is Julie Hagerty — a last-minute addition that CBS insists we see. Given that CBS requested her, I'm surprised she's not fat.

We go down one floor to the CBS "theater." The actors wait in the hall as the studio execs and we "producer types" walk past them and enter the room for the final showdown. Penny Marshall isn't coming, due to more dental work.

"Her entire family has bad teeth," says her company man, who, I can't help but notice, has a jacket over his arm and is sweating like a pig. I ask him what's wrong. He moves the coat and I see a video camera peeking out from under his arm.

"No! You can't!"

"I have to — or she'll fire me."

A video record of what a network president says about actors behind their backs? This is a first.

Jane freaks out that Les will cancel our pilot if he finds out. I worry Les will make a phone call and have us all killed. But this man, afraid of losing his job, is determined. My focus shifts from wondering how each actor will perform, to wondering how we can hide the video camera. I beg him, "At least sit way in the back of the theater in the dark."

"Good thinking," he says and scrambles to the top of the bleachers. He focuses his camera down on the tiny stage where the actors will be auditioning.

A half-second later, Les walks in with his entourage. I sneak a look back to see the red light of a camera.

"Light!" I whisper. "Light."

Penny's guy sneaks his thumb over the red light as the sweat drips off his nose.

The lights dim and we start with the role of Harvey. Peter Scolari and Michael McKean perform completely different takes on the character, and both are hilarious. Tough choice. I truly don't know which one I like better.

Les makes the decision for us this way: "Well … Peter's been very good to us. He's been on my network doing us favors in guest spots all season long. I'm tired of looking at him. Cast Michael. He's fresher."

We move on to the role of "Marion," Tom's daughter-in-law.

The girl reads. Les stops after her reading, turns around to Jane and yells, "Stop laughing, Jane."

At first we think he's joking, but Les continues. "I know what you're doing — laughing extra loud to influence my vote."

Jane says, "I'm laughing because I think she's funny."

Les says, "Yeah, right. Now stop it."

She stops it. We all stop it. No one dares make a peep at the next few actors, who seem extra tense at the vacuum of laughs they now face and all end up pushing too hard trying to make somebody laugh. No one does. I pray that the silence that greets them doesn't emphasize the sound of the video camera grinding away up in the back.

A woman enters to read for the role of Harvey's assistant, Jane. She asks which one Les is and then stupidly tries flirting with him from the stage, asking if she can have his pretty car. Les asks, "What do I get in return?" It's awkward and uncomfortable. And someone is in the back filming it.

The minute that Julie Hagerty walks into the room, I realize she's a perfect Jane. Perfect. I'm mad I never thought of her. Especially since *Lost in America* is one of my favorite movies.

McKean and Hagerty. So far, we're 2-for-2.

Les announces the show is skewing too old, and the next two roles should be cast as young as possible. It's the first time age has been brought up. It makes me nervous. The show takes place in a nursing home.

John Cygan (from *The Commish*) is cast as Tom's p-whipped son "Jeffrey." Natural. Funny. Handsome. An old friend from New Jersey. Another local boy made good. But John's only acceptable to Les if we agree to cast a certain actress as the wife — the youngest "Marion" we have. The girl's cute but completely wrong for the role. Les insists she's right. And she's young, which seems to be all that matters.

Now, if we can only find a leading man for the role of Tom.

* * *

For that we're down (or up) to Richard Mulligan (*Empty Nest*) and — well, nobody else. He's the last actor that CBS will approve to play the role — unless Matthau or Lemmon call up at the last minute.

There's only one problem. Olympia: "I'm not doing a show with Mulligan. I wouldn't even do a staged reading with him."

We decide to send her a reel of his work. Olympia agrees to meet with Richard at a lunch to see whether he'll be acceptable.

There's a hitch.

Richard won't meet with Olympia unless he has an offer to star in the series. Olympia won't let us offer him the role unless she meets him first. With Warner Bros. approval, we decide to hire him anyway and hope for the best. I hope to God we can sell Olympia on Richard Mulligan without her knowing he's already got the job.

In the restaurant, Jane changes tables three times to make sure everything is perfect. Finally she, Olympia, and I are put into a private room. Richard arrives. Tall. Gentlemanly. Nervous.

He begins to open up. He talks about everything, including the biggest love of his life — his old dog. A heartbreaking story. He tells us about working in England. Fondly remembering a small pub he used to go for a certain type of local beer that he's never seen since. The way he describes the beer I start to get thirsty, and I don't even drink beer. He's great. He's charming and funny, and a little sad.

We segue to working in television and *Waiting for God* in particular. As Richard talks, Olympia says nothing. I can't read her. Richard excuses himself to use the men's room. Olympia waits until he's out of earshot, and then leans in. I panic — afraid of what's about to come out of her mouth.

She says: "He's terrific. I'd be a fool not to work with him."

* * *

We take Olympia back to Warner to meet Andy Cadiff, her director. Both have theater backgrounds. Both are originally from Boston. Olympia is so friendly I can't believe she and Andy aren't old pals.

Andy leaves and Olympia, no longer animated, turns to me asking intently: "Who has the power in TV? The writer or the director?"

I happily tell her, "The writer."

"Then he'll be fine."

* * *

The day before we begin production, we have a secret reading of the script at Penny's house with the writers and the actors to make sure the actors get all the jokes and, most important, understand the characters they're playing and the timing of the scenes. It's a secret because if the studio knows where you're reading, they'll send someone who will then report any troubles back to their bosses and arm them with notes and ammunition for the official table-read note session.

Penny's house is a virtual museum. Every inch is covered with priceless art, Beanie Babies, bullet-art. And ashtrays. I finally understand why she offered her home. No one can ask her to put her cigarettes out in her own house.

In the reading, Richard Mulligan is perfection. Michael McKean also. Julie Hagerty also. John Cygan also. Olympia is stunned at the "polished performances."

As soon as the reading is over Penny bluntly starts giving notes. "Michael, talk faster." "Julie, I can't hear you." No subtlety here. But Penny's right on the money. A helpful shorthand. Like the way I talk to the actors in Jane's and my theater company back in New Jersey.

Olympia pulls me aside to tell me how amazing the others are. "Especially Mulligan." She adds that she's "thrilled to do this TV stuff with someone who's done it already and can walk me through it."

I love this woman. She's fun and down-to-earth. And what makes her funnier to me is she has the mouth of a truck driver. I'm going to love doing a series with her.

* * *

The table-read: Four hundred people gather on the soundstage. We're packed to the rafters with CBS brass, Warner people, our usual team of incredibly talented writer friends showing support, and my incredibly pregnant-with-twins wife whom I'm hoping won't go into labor until after we finish the reading.

I meet the British series creator Michael Aitkins, who has flown in from England to watch the "American television process." Will he like what we've done with his work? I'm more nervous about Michael being here than anyone. He's already proven this to be a hit show in England. If it fails in America, it'll be my fault, not his.

Les Moonves enters, followed by his entourage. That's our signal. The reading begins.

I welcome the cast and the Brit, and I intro our director.

We sit around the conference table. Penny lights up, breaking about a million fire codes.

It's a great read. Huge laughs. Everything works. Well, except for one small thing. The lovely little girl playing Marion. She seemed young before. Today she looks 12. Two words out of her mouth, and I realize we'll be recasting by the afternoon. She's paraphrasing, doing physical business (or trying to) as she sits at the long table. I'm not quite sure what she's doing.

A few times she actually tries grabbing at John Cygan to "do business" while he reads. She's talking in some bizarre half-British, half-Jersey accent. The panicked look on John's face says, "Look, pal. I know you're going down, but for God's sake don't take me with you!"

Les has only one note after the read. "It's great. Fire the girl." The CBS people leave.

Five minutes after the read, Jane and I are in the greenroom, me pacing — and Jane upset. We're so fixated on having to fire the poor girl we don't even realize we got zero notes from the network.

Jane asks, "What are you going to say?"

"I have no idea," I tell her, unaware until later that by her asking me that question she automatically made it my responsibility — a trick you'd think I'd stop falling for after 40 years.

"I'll just say something like: "We're going to have to let you go. It isn't your fault. The network wants to go in a different direction."

As I finish the last word, the poor doomed, fawn-like girl enters the room and sweetly asks, "Did you want to see me?" Not a clue this is coming.

I blurt out — as if I'm still rehearsing: "I'm sorry, but we're going to have to let you go... This isn't your fault... CBS wants to go in a different direction..."

She bursts into tears, collapses in my arms sobbing, before I finish firing her. "But I just quit my job!" she sobs. "They gave me a party!"

* * *

Over the next week we hear David Janollari give the same note in various forms, all with the same intent — disguise the fact that this is a show about senior citizens. From the abundance of "youthful notes" it's obvious this is a network mandate.

"Remove all references to age, death, and body parts."

"Can Richard Mulligan dye his hair brown?"

"Can Olympia and Richard rollerblade or do something else 'fun' in the boardwalk scene to explore the 'youthful fun' of the series?"

"The youthful what?" I ask.

"Youthful fun."

"The show takes place in a nursing home!"

"The signs all need to say Adult Community."

"The boardwalk scene's about two elderly people opening up and talking about their lives. The loss of his wife. Missed opportunity. The loss of her career."

"Fine, but can't they do it riding on a rollercoaster?"

* * *

We leave the note session and bump into Richard Mulligan, who thanks us for the opening day gift. We searched around England and tracked down the brand of beer he'd been pining for since his early pub days. British writer Michael Aitkins bought it for us personally and smuggled it into the country in his suitcase. Richard's touched.

Later that day we're told Richard is severely diabetic and has been on the wagon for years.

* * *

Two hours later. Penny calls the Writers' Room wondering where the new script pages are. We tell her we're too busy dodging phone calls like these to do any writing. She seems all right with it and goes off to sleep, wiped out from yet another dentist visit.

Back in the Writers' Room, Jane and I decide to put a stuffed bear on the bench next to Olympia and Richard in the boardwalk scene without changing one word of the script and hope that it looks "fun" enough.

* * *

Michael Aitkins is amazed at the workings of an American rewrite room. Having to listen to notes from people who aren't writers. Churning out entire scripts every single night after seeing what works and what doesn't work in the run-throughs. Having other writers there to help. In England, he writes the entire season of scripts by himself, then when he's finished, they bring the actors in and film them one after the other, like little plays. He gets no notes. No interference. No censors.

And according to him — no money.

* * *

The rewrite is finished. As the actors rehearse, Jane and I spend the rest of the day back in our office, Jane looking at gift baskets and reading good-luck cards. Me reading through the hundred or so British *Waiting for God* scripts and plotting out the entire first season with the best of the British storylines thinking this is without question the easiest pilot I've ever worked on.

We get a call to come down to the set.

* * *

We walk in to see our director blocking Michael McKean and Julie Hagerty in a scene: "OK, Michael, in this scene, you'll enter from over there." Andy points to the door on the left.

Behind his back, I see Penny shaking her head no, and pointing to the other entrance on the right. Michael nods to Penny and goes to where Penny told him to go, completely ignoring Andy.

Unaware of what's going on behind him, Andy says, "No, I'm sorry, Michael." And indicates the other door. "From over *there*."

Then I hear Penny's voice muttering loudly, "But it's funnier from over *there*."

Andy diplomatically switches the entrance to the way Penny wants it. He politely excuses himself from the actors, crosses over to me, and announces he's quitting.

Richard Mulligan wanders over: "She's been doing this all day. One more time, and *I'm* out of here."

Jane's personality changes from beach bunny to pit bull. "Penny, what are you doing? You can't direct the scenes. We have a director."

Penny says, "I know, but the little guy told me to come down here and do this."

"What little guy?"

"You know, the little idiot."

We realize she means David Janollari.

Jane calls "the little guy."

"You idiot. Did you tell Penny to re-direct all of Andy's work?"

He laughs like a little kid with his hand in the cookie jar. "Hey. She's a famous director — why not use her?"

Jane says, "You almost shut down the show, you asshole" and hangs up.

We ask Penny to stop. Andy is happy. Richard is happy. Penny couldn't care less. But we keep the entrance the way she wanted it. Because Penny was right. It was funnier her way.

Back on the set we see Olympia walking like Tim Conway's Old Man from a *Carol Burnett Show* sketch. I ask Andy what's going on.

He tells me, "Olympia is discovering the role."

"Why is she walking like that?"

"Because she's supposed to be old. She also wants to use a cane."

I panic at CBS's youthful reaction to an old lady with a cane.

I ask Olympia if she is serious about the cane. She says yes. The lady in the British show used a cane. "And if I'm going to play a woman who's only in this home because of her bad hip I'm using a fucking cane!"

I start to walk away, and she calls after me: "And I'm wearing a wig, too!"

From behind the set, I hear David Janollari mutter: "Not unless it's sexy and blonde!"

* * *

At one point in the middle of the run-through, Olympia breaks down crying.

The idea of being performance-level ready from Day One is mind-blowing to Olympia. She's a stage actress who is used to discovering the character as she goes and not being ready until the time the curtain goes up opening night. TV acting requires you to be ready from Day One.

She pounds her chest and screams at the top of her lungs: "I am bereft of my process!"

Everyone moves away.

Jane says to me: "Did she just use the word 'bereft?' Does she know she's doing television?"

I try to calm Olympia down. She shrugs me off. "I'll be fine. Let's just do it."

Olympia's husband — the brilliant actor Louis Zorich — tells her: "Just say your lines as Olympia. You're in your own way."

The next day, that's exactly what she does, and he's right. She's great.

* * *

Opening night. Shooting the show before 300 excited fans. We limit the number of agents allowed in the building, because they never laugh at tapings. They only sit there trying to make deals.

Jane is stationed in the greenroom with the network and studio executives to keep them out of the director's hair and let me know "their thoughts" by calling me on a telephone after each take.

I'm on the floor with the cameras, making sure our angles all work, watching the performances, and listening to audience reaction.

Penny goes back and forth from the floor to the greenroom. She also took the time before anyone arrived to personally copy and decorate the greenroom with an article from *The New York Times* about how much spending money older TV viewers have.

We start filming the show. Olympia makes her entrance, and the audience cheers wildly — clapping and stomping its feet. Richard Mulligan makes his entrance, and the audience cheers again.

Inside the greenroom, Les Moonves and the studio people sit watching the show on monitors. They look at each other befuddled. "Why is the audience cheering like that?"

Penny enters and lights up a cigarette, turning the greenroom into a smoking car with no ventilation.

Les asks, "Penny, why are they cheering like that out there?"

She says, "I have no idea."

She puts her cigarette out and excuses herself, trapping the death cloud of smoke inside the little makeshift room. She returns to the soundstage, where she stands in front of the bleachers and encourages the audience to stamp their feet and cheer when Michael McKean and Julie Hagerty make *their* entrances.

The show could not go more smoothly, but pilot shoots being what they are, everyone has an opinion. Jane calls me on the soundstage after every scene to report the execs' reactions.

"Billy, they want to know if you can get Olympia to say that line with more of a smile."

"Tell them to go screw themselves. The scene was great."

Jane, to "the suits" who requested the change: "Billy said they shot it that way this afternoon."

* * *

At 10 p.m. — incredibly early by pilot standards, which usually go into the wee small hours of the morning — a man enters from the greenroom. Penny's leftover smoke billows out behind him, like he's stepping out of a burning building. He finds Penny and me and asks that we reshoot one of the scenes again, because he thought Richard could be better.

"Let's do it again, and this time…."

Penny loses it in front of the audience.

"Are you an idiot? Richard Mulligan is a sick man. He has diabetes. You want to kill him? What's wrong with you? Are you an asshole? Get out of here! And who the hell are you, anyway?"

Trying not to cry, the man answers: "I'm…I'm, uh, Head of Comedy Development for CBS."

Penny, nice as can be: "Oh. Very nice to meet you."

The Head of Comedy goes back into the greenroom to sit in the cloud of Penny's trapped smoke. And we don't reshoot a thing.

* * *

Editing this show is fun. Everything works. Andy filmed a great show. The actors were on the money. I couldn't be prouder.

Penny doesn't need to see any more dentists by the time we start the edit. She's always with us in the editing room. And she's so sharp it's scary. Her guy says, "Her movies are made in the editing room," as if it's the company slogan.

A sound effect of an engine starting up takes too long to get from the studio library to our editing room. Penny hands the man from her company her portable DAT machine ("I never go anywhere without it." — or words to that effect) and sends him out to the parking lot to start up his car and record it for our show. The sound of his car is edited into the pilot before the sound effect from the studio library ever arrives.

At one point, Penny suggests cutting in a different angle in one scene. I like the scene the way it is, so I try telling her we tried it her way earlier and it didn't work, so we're leaving the cut the way it is.

I leave the room to get my eighth Coke of the day. When I return three minutes later, I see she's had the editor redo the cut her way. "See? Wur fah…" And damn if she isn't right. It does wur fah.

* * *

With the final edited version, we go down to the "Warner Bros. Testing Center," where people are dragged in from a local mall for something like $50 apiece in exchange for viewing and rating our show.

Penny's already there when I arrive. Her assistant is beside her, holding her ashtray.

Jane makes the comment she makes at every one of these tests. "If testing worked, every show on TV would be a hit." Luckily, the man conducting the testing isn't here this time to be told how stupid his job is.

The audience watches the show, unaware of what it's about to see or who's involved. We watch through monitors in another room. If they like what they see, they'll turn a dial to the right. If they dislike what they see, they'll turn it to the left.

I've never seen the dials turned as high to the right.

Everyone loves it.

A teenager says what she likes best is that the old guy and the old lady are rebellious and defy authority. It's the reason the show was a hit with teenagers in England even though it starred senior citizens. I wish Les Moonves was sitting here to hear it.

The man conducting the test asks the group, "Would you watch this show?"

Everyone loudly says, "Yes!"

"Anything you didn't like?"

"Just one thing," says one woman. "Every time people walk in the door, the audience applauds. I mean, what is this, *Laverne & Shirley*?"

Laverne sucks on her cigarette and glares at the TV monitor.

* * *

As a result of the testing, we get notes from CBS to take all the applause out of the show. The note says, "This is not 1975!" Penny thinks they are idiots.

It doesn't bother me — the applause shows the audience likes the actors — which should be a good thing. And we're not trying to fool anyone into thinking that there's not an audience in the studio watching us film the show. You hear them laughing, don't you? However, if it means getting the show on the air, I'll cut out whatever they like.

It turns out we can't take out the audio of Richard Mulligan's applause because there's dialogue over it and Richard's unavailable to do any looping, so it's decided by Les Moonves that we can keep Richard and Olympia's applause, but will have to cut out Julie Hagerty's and Michael McKean's and rerecord their lines.

And I get to tell them.

At the recording studio. Michael McKean puts on headphones and goes into the booth. I speak to him over an intercom.

"Michael…my first note is…we need to rerecord your first line."

Over a microphone from the booth, his voice asks, "Why?"

"Well, because CBS wants the applause removed."

There is a slight pause.

The voice asks, "Are you taking out Richard and Olympia's applause?"

"Uh…no."

"What's your *second* note?"

* * *

Before we turn in the final show, there is a mandate from CBS. Change the title to something "younger." And pay someone to "paint box" the film, literally changing all the signs on the set that say "Rest Home" to "Retirement Community."

And *Waiting for God* becomes *Alive and Kicking*.

* * *

We might as well have titled it *Dead on Arrival*.

A series starring Academy Award winner Olympia Dukakis, multiple Emmy Award winner Richard Mulligan, *Spinal Tap's* Michael McKean, and *Airplane's* Julie Hagerty. Based on a wildly popular British sitcom classic. Produced by director/comedienne Penny Marshall. Brought to you by Warner Bros. — the biggest supplier of sitcoms in the industry. Directed by Andy Cadiff, who made *Home Improvement* a top-10 hit for all of its eight years. Written and produced by Jane and me. For CBS, the network with the largest 50-plus-year-old audience. How could we miss?

Like this: Les Moonves read a *New York Times* article that accused CBS of pandering to old people. As a result, he picked up only one older-skewing show for the season — opting for Bob Newhart's show *George & Leo.* I'm happy for Mr. Newhart. But couldn't they pick up two? We would have made a good hour together.

Instead they pay off Olympia Dukakis for a guaranteed six-episode commitment, Richard Mulligan for a guaranteed six-episode commitment, Penny Marshall for a guaranteed six-episode commitment, and Jane and me for a guaranteed six-episode commitment.

For 10 cents more we could have filmed the entire first season.

* * *

I call Olympia in New Jersey. She is crushed and angry. She spends the following summer directing our hotel sex farce *Do Not Disturb* after the theater turns down her first choice — *Antigone*.

* * *

The last call I make is to Penny, who says, "Fnahhhkaa…"
I couldn't agree more.

GOOD GOOGA MOOGA

"The Hughleys"

My twin sons are born, and my life completely changes. Whatever came before is now irrelevant and unimportant. I never knew I could love anyone as much as I love these boys. And so I segue from running and creating my own shows to consulting one or two days a week on other people's shows, because I simply never want to leave the house.

My favorite of the consulting jobs is *The Hughleys,* starring one of the "Kings of Comedy," DL Hughley. Based on his life, the show is about a black man (DL) who moves to an all-white neighborhood and is afraid his children will lose their identities — instead of what knowing it's like to grow up black, they'll find themselves only *Black*ish*. Yes, I used that word on purpose.

The greatest part of consulting on someone else's show is you have no responsibility. You get paid a lot of money to show up, do as you're asked to fix the scripts, and go home. It's all somebody else's problem.

The bad part, which I don't realize until years later, is that everyone forgets you ever knew how to executive produce a show. It becomes an uphill battle to get back into that game.

However, *The Hughleys* is a fantastic place to work, with a terrific writing staff and a great star setting the pace for the fun-but-professional atmosphere. I also get to work with guest stars Sherman Hemsley (*The Jeffersons*), Marla Gibbs (*The Jeffersons*), Pat Morita (*The Karate Kid*), Billy Dee Williams (*Star Wars*), Virginia Capers (Broadway's

Raisin), John Astin (*The Addams Family*), model Tyra Banks, John Hamm (*Mad Men*), Oscar-winner Mo'Nique (*Precious*), Fred Willard (what isn't he in?), singer Kelly Rowland, and a lot of other apparently famous musicians I'd never heard of.

The staff is fun, and the producers let us try a lot of different things. We cover dyslexia, interracial dating, drugs, adoption, guns in the home, how to handle discovering your friend is friends with a racist, sexual orientation, and — in one episode — black families having to continually see white Santa Clauses everywhere.

In one of our Christmas shows, DL protests his kids' school forcing a white Santa Claus on his children, so the school's parents get together and agree to have a multicultural Christmas instead, swearing to honor *everyone's* holiday traditions.

Trouble comes when the Dutch family down the street wants to include Zwarte Piet. In Holland, as it turns out, Sinterklaas (a benevolent *white* saint) lives not at the North Pole but in Spain, and he has a black slave named Zwarte Piet (Black Pete) — played by a white guy in blackface with big lips.

Wait, it gets better: Zwarte Piet carries a large sack so the black man can terrify the naughty white children when he takes them away forever for being bad.

It's moments like this when I play up my mother's Italian heritage and completely ignore my father's Dutch lineage.

* * *

My favorite moment of the series is the musical-spoof of *Jack and the Beanstalk*, performed like a Disney special. The production value is terrific. Jane and I write the script and the lyrics to all the songs but one, penned by our show's creator, Matt Wickline. Our show's composer, Paul Buckley, writes the music.

Only after the script is written and the music is composed do we discover everyone in our cast sings. We figured someone would have checked that out before we started, but ... Phew!

Every department goes above and beyond to make it a truly special event.

And for a week it's like Jane and I are back in New Jersey doing our children's theater — in fact, using some of the exact same jokes. A big production number "Sell the Cow" is done a la "Be Our Guest" from *Beauty and the Beast,* with DL fake-tap-dancing to sound effects on a tabletop as dancers and gymnasts twirl and kick around him. It's fantastic. (And luckily still available on You Tube.)

This episode could have been a TV special on its own. I wish we'd done more like this.

* * *

When you're away from a show and step in sporadically, as consultants do, things that you would've gotten used to had you been there full-time stick out like sore thumbs.

For instance, a lot of TV shows use Little People as stand-ins for the children in the cast. Kids can only work so many hours a day, so the Little People can step in to read their lines in rehearsal if the kids are in school, and they're also the right height to check lighting, etc. Best, they work adult hours.

To show up for a run-through and see a tender scene between a father and son played by six-foot Eric Kramer with a 30-year-old Little Person sitting on his knee talking baby talk is just, well, weird.

And when a network exec tells you he doesn't think that scene works, your only answer is, "No kidding."

* * *

One of our Little Person stand-ins is referred to in the Writers' Room as "Eight Days," because at one rehearsal, out of the blue, our producer says: "Look how big that guy's head is. I bet it would take eight days to saw through that."

For the rest of the series the man is known behind his back as "Eight Days."

* * *

A practical joke we enjoy pulling is convincing producer John Bowman, who barely learns anyone's names, that our accountant is really twins. The guy walks by the Writers' Room, and John, trying hard to be better at memorizing crew names, asks if that's "Daniel." We say no, that's his twin brother "Paul." Later he asks if the same guy is Paul, and we tell him no, that's Daniel. We get away with this for two years.

* * *

Writer John Beck is dared to drink an entire bottle of honey for $100. He does, wins the money, and spends the rest of the day vomiting.

* * *

After being cooped up in the Writers' Room for a late rewrite and hating the stuffy air and smell of take-out food, one of our execs throws a chair through the sealed closed window. The breeze is lovely.

Just another day on *The Hughleys*.

* * *

Not every day we walk into the show is fun-loving. I clearly remember DL chasing producer David Janollari around parked cars in the lot screaming at him to go fuck himself and trying to punch him in the face after David suggests, in an attempt to speed up the production day, that DL stop putting twists in his hair.

David isn't seen on the set much for the remainder of the year. DL's hair doesn't change.

* * *

Despite four years and a loyal following, the show is canceled.

DL continues to become one of the biggest names in stand-up.

And when a terrific show called *Black-ish* airs, winning all sorts of well-deserved awards, I find I'm the only one looking around, scratching my head, and asking, "Hey, doesn't anybody remember *The Hughleys?*"

"THE BILLION-DOLLAR INDUSTRY"

Writing porno for CBS

After scouring all the comedy clubs for the next big sitcom star, we find ourselves howling at this short man with dark, curly hair in a bowling shirt and vest who fires off jokes and bits like a machine gun for an hour and a half straight. There isn't a chance to come up for air. I have no idea how his mind can race this fast. Why isn't this guy a huge star? We ask if we can write a show for him for CBS.

"Yes!"

* * *

Jane and I have lunch with him at the ultra-hip Mondrian Hotel on the Sunset Strip. It's supposed to be a "meet and greet" lunch to see if we hit it off with him, and he with us. We talk about his career, shows we've worked on, comics we all know. He has several premise ideas for shows to star himself. We have some better ones that actually make sense. He talks about how he thinks *The Drew Carey Show* is a hit because Bruce Helford drove across the country with Drew while they were creating the show and spent every waking hour together.

I suggest, "Or maybe Bruce Helford wrote a good show."

He tells us about a series he did several years ago. He explains the horrendous working conditions. "The writers wouldn't listen to me. They would only allow me three notes per script, and I had to write them down and hand them in. I wasn't even allowed to voice my opinion on my own show."

"What assholes." I say. "Jane and I work very closely with the comedians we write for. You have to listen to them. Nobody knows what makes them funnier than they do themselves."

Five hours later, I mention that I have to go.

"Already? What for?"

"I have to pick up my kids."

"Can't someone else go?"

"Uh…no."

We get up to leave. He says to Jane, "You have to go, too?"

"Uh…same car."

* * *

Deal in place, Jane and I get together at the man's Hollywood Hills bachelor pad. It's decorated in black leather, glass tables, a massive fish tank, and lots of comedy awards. He chain-smokes but is polite enough to do it at a window by a fan — which blows the secondhand smoke toward his neighbor's house.

Again he suggests we spend every waking moment together. I assure him, "We'll have everything we need to showcase you in two or three sessions."

He stares at me, confused.

He shows us file after file of jokes, categorized according to subject.

We order lunch as he does more routines we didn't get to see at the comedy club. There's no denying his talent. He's amazing.

The premise we come up with is simple, he'll play a Howard Stern-like radio host, which will give him ample opportunity to do his eclectic comedy pieces and riffs on various topics. He'll be single, so we can incorporate his many dating routines. And there will be fantasy scenes that play out some of his thoughts on women and dating.

Seems cut and dried.

* * *

That night the faxes begin. Page after page after page. Notes, thoughts, ideas, joke pitches, parts of his routines that could be whole episodes, episode ideas, casting suggestions. Jane's glad he doesn't have her fax number.

* * *

At our second session he pulls out file folders that contain his thoughts on the series. We're handed a 30-page document that contains rules on how to write the show.

No. 1: "I should be the funniest person in the show."

No. 2: "I should have the funniest lines."

It goes downhill from there.

* * *

When he leaves the room for a smoke, Jane suggests we back out of this project. Funny, Adrienne had suggested the same thing after the previous night's 10th fax at 3 a.m. ruined what was otherwise a fun night.

"Come on," I say, "He's just excited. I like that he's passionate. It'll be fine."

After 10 hours, we're ready to leave for the day. Our star is surprised.

"Already? Let's have dinner and keep working."

"Oh, I can't. My wife's waiting for me."

"Jane?"

"His wife's waiting for me, too."

* * *

We pitch the show to Paramount. They love it. They'll set up a meeting for us to pitch the show to CBS for the following week. We walk out to the courtyard after the meeting. I'm happy about how things went. It's a good show and a great showcase for our star.

We step out into the sun.

Our star lights up a cigarette and turns to us. "You want to go first, or shall I?"

"Go first for what?"

"To talk about what just went on in there."

"What do you mean?"

"I think you could have done better."

"What do you mean? We just sold the show. They're very excited."

"Yes, but I don't think we should settle. Do you?"

* * *

That night. More faxes explaining how to fine-tune our pitch. He suggests we change him from a radio DJ to an Internet DJ. Keep in mind the Internet had barely been invented at this point. No one would know what he was talking about. He also suggests we add a series regular girlfriend character. I call him back in the morning and explain why we want to keep him single and why Paramount agrees that's the best way to showcase his talents. The wealth of his stand-up material is from a single guy's POV. I assure him we know what we're doing.

He explains, "Yes, but on my last show I had no girlfriend, and the whole thing imploded. So maybe I need a girlfriend."

I'm starting to guess why the last show imploded.

* * *

At CBS, we sell the show in about five minutes. And it's on my birthday. Happy birthday to me. They love the premise and love our star. To please him, I cram in the fact that his radio show would also be simulcast on the Internet. It's the only part of the pitch they ask us to take out. ("What is that Internet crap you're talking about? It's stupid.")

The next step is to write up a two-page synopsis of the pilot storyline we've sold and send it to CBS for their official approval, so we can start writing the script.

We step out of CBS's Television City into the late afternoon shadows. Our star is clearly upset. I expect he's embarrassed at the Internet suggestion. But that's not it. He's mad.

"They're wrong. The next wave of radio is the Internet."

"Not at CBS it isn't. Not today. This is the audience that watches Angela Lansbury solve murders. Those people can't even work their VCRs."

Jane reminds him again, "And they just bought the show!" Rather than get excited at the sale, he suggests we go back to his house and start working on the pilot script. I explain it's my birthday and I'm going to dinner with my wife.

"Do you have to go tonight?"

* * *

We agree to meet on the weekend. I scribble up the storyline we've sold and present it to him Saturday morning so he can throw in some jokes and we can have this to CBS by Monday. When Jane and I enter his house, we see that he is visibly upset.

"What's wrong now?"

"I think I should have a girlfriend on the show."

"CBS doesn't want a girlfriend. They specifically said they didn't want that."

"But if I have a girlfriend it'll be better."

"How is that better? You won't be able to do half the stuff we talked about."

"Tim Allen has a wife on his show."

"We're not doing Tim Allen's show."

I hand him what Jane and I wrote. It captures his talent perfectly. It's everything we talked about. He reads it, combing over every syllable with a serious face. He takes his time and writes notes in the margins.

Jane and I sit for an hour and shoot each other looks as he pores over the two-page, double-spaced outline. It's going to be a long day.

* * *

"I have a better idea than this," he finally says, literally putting our work into a garbage can. "You know how pornography is a billion-dollar business?"

"Excuse me?" I ask as I look at our work, which is now lying in the trash.

"It's true. Everyone in the country is into pornography."

Jane asks, "They are?"

"Yes. What if my girlfriend and I realize we can't have sex without our pornography and have to wean ourselves off it?"

"For the pilot episode you want to do this?"

"Yes."

"At CBS?"

"Yeah, and I can walk over to a big bookcase and open it up and we see I have, like, ten thousand porno videos. That'll be hilarious."

Jane's eyes widen when she notices the big bookcase across the room.

"But … you don't have a girlfriend in the show!"

"That's why it's better if I do. Otherwise the porno thing won't work."

* * *

Two weeks later. We're still arguing about the pilot storyline — the one we already sold, the one that already works, the one that contains our star doing more funny things per square inch than any comedian on the air. Paramount keeps calling asking for the two-page "beat sheet." I don't want to alert them to a potential disaster, so I try to explain that our comedian is simply being picky because he feels this is his big shot.

Paramount faxes him to "let the writers write."

To get around Paramount's request, instead of sending us endless faxes with ideas and notes and jokes on them, he sends us endless faxes with ideas and notes and jokes on them labeled "Top Secret."

* * *

I suggest to Jane, "Let's just write his porno outline and get it over with."

I take out a legal pad and let our star dictate his show. It's incomprehensible.

He loves it. If it's this hard to get the pilot storyline done, how do we do this on a weekly basis without driving ourselves nuts, if the show ends up on the fall schedule? We decide to give both outlines (ours, and the porno outline) to Paramount.

* * *

We get a call from Paramount the next day.

"This is a joke, right?"

I explain the situation.

"I'm not sending this to CBS."

"He claims the porno business is a billion-dollar business."

"Not at CBS it isn't."

* * *

Our star thinks the woman from Paramount doesn't like it because she's a prude. He swears she has big stashes of porno in her house but won't admit it, and that we're all wrong.

We go to her boss at Paramount with the problem.

"What is he, an idiot?"

A conference call is initiated by Paramount over the Christmas holidays, with Jane and me and our star on the line at our various homes.

Paramount: "Is everyone here?"

Everyone else: "Yes/Yeah/Here."

Paramount: "Here's the thing. We love what Billy and Jane came up with. It showcases you so well and…"

It's the last word the man gets to say. Our star goes on about porno and wanting a girlfriend on the show and that the only person Jane and I have to please is him.

Paramount finally gets a word in. "Can I say something? One thing. Just one thing. Can I say one thing?"

"Sure, what is it?"

"This conversation is over."

Paramount hangs up.

Jane's phone rings a minute later. It's Paramount.

"Life is too short. I'm killing this project. But we love you guys. Let's roll over your deal and you can do a show for someone else next season."

* * *

A week later we get a call from our star.

"OK, I'll do it your way."

"Excuse me?"

"I'll do it your way."

"It's too late. Paramount moved on. CBS moved on. You don't trust us. You don't like what we wanted to do."

"I know, but I'll do it, even if I think it stinks!"

We pass.

* * *

He's still one of the best stand-up comics I'll ever see. But sometimes there's a reason they don't have their own shows.

IT'S NOT YOU, IT'S US

"Yes, Dear"

Yes, Dear is the first show I have no idea how to write. Not a clue.

Greg Garcia, who wrote *Family Guy* (and eventually *Raising Hope* and *My Name is Earl*) and our friend Alan Kirschenbaum created the show. The staff is good. The actors are good — especially Liza Snyder (*Man of the House*) and Mike O'Malley (*Sully, Glee,* and co-author of the Broadway musical *Escape to Margaritaville*). Yes, everybody on the show is good. But Jane and I are not.

Yes, Dear is a kind of throwback to shows from the 1960s where husbands are afraid of their wives. God forbid the women find out the men want to play golf, etc.

I just don't find it funny. I don't understand why the guys can't talk to their wives. After I complain once too often about it, one of the staff members says, "Oh, that's right, Billy. You *like* going home to your wife." I have no answer for that.

I try to make a go of it. But having written for *The Hughleys* for the past few years, I also have the cadence of DL's voice and those scripts stuck in my head, so when we try writing a *Yes, Dear*, it doesn't come out right. The jokes we write are too snarky, and the rhythms are wrong. And when Greg Garcia says he wants to tell a story a certain way and I innocently say, "Or you could do it the funny way," I think I've sealed our doom.

It doesn't help that Jane is going through an ugly divorce. When we are there on one of our two consulting days each week, she is a mess — constantly leaving the room to cry — and I am completely lost with what makes this show tick, and therefore I'm completely useless to the process. And, frankly, Greg and Alan are paying us way too much money for any of that.

After the season ends, we have a big wrap party at a hip Hollywood pool hall, where Greg and I play eight-ball all night long. Maybe 10 straight games.

The next morning, Alan calls me in to say Greg is firing us. I'm not at all surprised. I ask, "Is it because I beat him at pool?"

No. It's what I thought — the Jane's-going-through-a-divorce-and-absent-too-much-and-Billy-looks-down-on-the-show-and-thinks-he's-the-funniest-guy-in-the-room-and-likes-to-go-home-to-his-wife-and-kids-thing.

Once we are let go, we immediately go from being two of CBS's favorite writers where we sell a pilot almost every season, to "Nah." Overnight.

Being unemployed in Los Angeles, a place that identifies you only by your latest job, is brutal. Worse than being shunned, we are invisible.

I'm told by a good source that it even happened to Lucille Ball. After the failure of *Life with Lucy,* Aaron Spelling pretended not to see her in a restaurant.

This is the time you need support the most. Luckily Jane and I are here for each other to get through this ugly patch.

We jump back into the theater and produce two more Off-Broadway shows: Jane and I star in *Silent Laughter*, performing a slapstick silent-film comedy live on stage, complete with Wurlitzer organ and title cards above the actors' heads; and *The Property Known as Garland*, which I write for Adrienne, about Judy Garland's last concert appearance in Copenhagen; Jane and I always have a few projects going at once. When one doesn't work out, we jump to the next one.

After *Yes, Dear,* Jane divorces her husband and regains her sanity and health. Once immersed in the theater again, we eventually get our writing groove back. But returning to television isn't easy. The faces at the networks and studios change so fast that if you "consult" a couple of days a week, the new people have no idea you once knew how to "exec produce." And if you go off to produce Off-Broadway plays in New York, they don't even remember you know how to "consult."

Never leave your base, young writers! That's the lesson we learned here. But Jane and I needed it to clear our heads and regroup.

I don't regret scaling back my show-running days to be a two or three day a week consultant for other people's shows so I could be there for my children. Not for a second. But it probably wasn't the smartest career move.

At the start of the following season of *Yes, Dear,* I happen to be on the lot selling another show and sneak into the *Yes, Dear* Writers' Room while the staff is out to lunch. I go to the whiteboard that hangs in every Writers' Room and write a note to Greg Garcia, who has still not talked to me since our firing.

"Hi Greg. We haven't heard from you for some reason. Shouldn't we be starting the new season soon? Let us know. Billy and Jane."

Then I sneak out as Greg and the writers return from their break to see my message on the wall. I think it's the only laugh I ever got out of Greg.

Jane gets a little more out of it than I do. Ten years later, at the height of the market, Greg buys her beach house.

"THERE GOES MY CHILDHOOD"

Disney and "Jack and Janet Save the Planet"

"The people at Disney want to see you."

I swear our agent is playing a joke. We wrote for Martin Lawrence, Don Rickles, and Andrew "Dice" Clay. Take a meeting at Disney?

We take a meeting at Disney. The building where we meet is cold and sterile and corporate, except for the pictures of Mickey Mouse and brightly colored posters for their TV shows that take up all the wall space. They tell us what they're looking for, based on detailed research.

Today's kids are the ones who will save the planet. Disney wants us to target the "green" kids out there who are trying to make a difference. Jane asks, "Oh, you mean like "Janet Saves the Planet?" Jane tells about her environmentally friendly sister Janet, who was on a crusade to save the planet and gave everyone reusable water bottles as Christmas presents. But the bottles were wrapped in enough tissue, cardboard, and wrapping paper to level a rain forest.

We laugh, thank them for the meeting, and tell them we'll think about it. Five minutes later, in the car, our agent calls to say we sold the show.

"What show?"

"Janet Saves the Planet."

Since it's sold, Jane and I go back to our office to figure out what "it" is. After looking at a detailed PowerPoint presentation of Disney's environmental research, we settle on a girl who's a good-hearted crusader who always goes too far, resulting in — you guessed it — hilarity. Jane and I make a pact that we're not going to write what we see as the norm in current children's shows: loud obnoxious shows with ridiculous overacting and noise, with jokes that don't fit the characters coming out of kids' mouths. We'll write outrageous stuff, but it will come from believable characters who talk like normal kids. We're asked to add a brother character to get more boys to watch. We do. The show becomes *Jack and Janet Save the Planet.*

Not only is this a fun script to write, but we have such a good time doing it that, on our own, we quickly start working on an entire season's worth of shows and start writing pieces of those, too. We turn in the first draft of the pilot — and our enthusiasm is not shared.

"Where are the jokes?"

I say there are six on the first page. I guess they can't see them, because they aren't written like joke-jokes. They come from character. Only when we hold auditions and the execs hear the dialogue out loud do they realize how big the laughs are.

We use scenes from a few other episodes for the actors to audition with, as well, to give us more variety in the audition "sides" but mainly so Jane and I can hear the dialogue and go back and tweak the next three episodes. If this show goes forward, we'll have four scripts ready to go.

We flip over 11-year-old China Anne McClain, a Judy Taylor casting agent find who has the timing of a 40-year-old comedy pro. We've found our Janet. And she's better than we'd hoped for.

As Janet's tech-savvy sidekick "Mookie," we cast Jake Short, another kid with old-school comic timing. Jake has obviously studied the great silent-screen comedians. When I ask if he has any questions about the scene he's about to audition with, he asks if I want a "slow burn" after a particular line, or a "double take," or a "deadpan" expression.

As the parents we cast Elise Neal (*The Hugbleys*) as Janet's mother and Larry Poindexter (he's on TV everywhere) as Jack's father. Without making a thing out of it, they will be one of the first interracial couples to ever appear on the Disney Channel. Nice!

The plot of the pilot is wildly ambitious. Janet and her friends decide to build a wind turbine on the roof of their Manhattan building. They do, and it's so strong it blows the dog (and wig) of the building's most hated resident right off the roof and onto the ledge of the building across the street (shades of Buster Keaton's *Steamboat Bill Jr.*).

The kids have to get into that building and retrieve the dog before its owner wakes up from her sunbathing nap. Once out on the ledge of the building across the street, Janet reenacts silent comedy star Harold Lloyd's *Safety Last* famous bit hanging off the side of a building 30 floors above the street, as she tries to save the dog. Then after a series of setbacks, Janet finally retrieves the dog — but out of the blue it's snatched out of her hands by a red-tailed hawk that swoops in for some lunch. And finally, when we think all is lost, the hawk drops the dog back into the arms of Janet, who safely returns it to her owner before the nasty old lady even notices he's missing.

China's great with the physical comedy, and Jake knows how to take a hit and knock himself out. These kids are fun.

Our old children's theater scripts had jokes for the adults as well as the kids. We try to do the same thing here, but Disney isn't interested in those kinds of jokes. Out they come. The only sort of risqué thing we get away with is when the villainess of the show is out sunbathing and rises with an open robe right in the eye-line of Mookie, who takes one look and mutters, "There goes my childhood." Great joke. (Not mine — thank you, writer Myles Mapp.)

My sons come to the set one day. Incredibly handsome twin boys (just being factual). And Disney likes twins. The boys meet the Disney folks, who start to ask questions. Do you sing? Yes. Do you play instruments? Yes. Before they can offer them their own show, William cuts them off with the fact he wouldn't be interested. I wonder how often that happens.

Luckily we can't use stunt people for this crazy episode because they'd never match the kids. Fine with me. I like to see actors take their own falls. And I like physical comedy in one take. I don't think faked gags are funny. If an actor looks like he's really in danger or has genuinely hurt himself, it's always funnier.

There are a few complications working out physical comedy with kids. Legally, the skyscraper ledge our characters are afraid of falling off can only be so many inches above the ground in real life, making it hard to shoot. And the ledge needs a lip on it because we can't make it look too scary or the kids at home will be too scared.

Jane and I never used to think about safety when we were producing and acting in our early plays. If I had to soar above the stage attached to helium balloons (twice: *Silent Laughter* and *What the Bellhop Saw*), I just held on to the rope.

In our musical *Merrily We Dance and Sing* (*The Naughty Boy*), Jane had to fall backward from the set's second story into a crash pad backstage. When she balked, claiming it was unsafe, I told her there was nothing to it and climbed the ladder to demonstrate how safe it was. But once I got up there and looked down at the crash pad from the platform above, I said, "Yeah, you'll be fine," and climbed back down the ladder. That was good enough for Jane, who did it every performance.

But here at Disney, having to deal with kids and insurance, we suddenly have to act responsibly.

This was an overly ambitious project that we pull off due to the kids' professionalism, our director Shelley Jensen (*Fresh Prince of Bel Air*, *Friends*, and our own *Wayans Bros.*) knowing how to shoot it, and producer Frank Pace never saying no to us.

Frank is our kind of producer. If we say we want to have a red-tailed hawk swoop in and snatch a dog out of a kid's arms, while she's hanging from a pipe 30 stories above the street, with a wind machine that blows everything off a roof, he says OK and then gets it done. None of this, "The problem with that is..." which we've heard from other producers.

I never want to know why we can't do something. I just want it done. Frank gets it done — and somehow does it under budget. I'm sure we frustrate him, but he never shows it. He's that good.

Not only does Frank watch the budget, he also watches the clock. (Kids can work only so many hours.) To save us time on a special effect that's taking too long, Frank quickly grabs a bowl of Cool Whip and a spoon and climbs a ladder and flings "bird droppings" on our villainess. Perfect aim, too.

The end product is better than we had hoped for. The kids in the testing center howl with laughter as they view the pilot. We see a long life ahead of us. We couldn't be more thrilled. China and Jake will be on the air for years.

They are. But not in our show. Disney doesn't pick up *Jack and Janet Save the Planet*.

We're told that despite testing higher than *Hannah Montana,* further research said kids would prefer hearing someone sing than watching someone recycle trash.

"But you told us this is what you wanted."

"Yes, but further research told us kids prefer singing."

We're told our show didn't hit any of the four Disney "quadrants" for success. A show needs music, live performance, recording, and merchandise. No characters in our episode sang, so that eliminated music, recording, and touring. And the only potential merchandising would be reusable water bottles — excessive wrapping sold separately.

Unfortunately, "Janet" didn't save any planets. Instead, "Janet," "Mookie," and their friend "Molly" became the cast of *A.N.T. Farm*. And "Jack" wound up on *Lab Rats*.

We hear from several writers that in the years that follow, our teleplays are given out as examples of how to write a good script. So we've got that going for us.

Jane fares better than me on this one. She walks away from the show with her own happy ending and the love of her life — our director, Shelley Jensen.

THE TAG

Still at it

And that's where my TV journals end.

Jane and I take a six-year break from TV to do our Off-Broadway run and national tour of *You've Got Hate Mail* — the story of a woman (Jane) who discovers her husband (me) is cheating through an email he writes to his mistress that accidentally goes to the wife's address. (Hmm, where'd we get that idea from?)

During this time, the television world goes on without us. Four million additional channels open up. Movie stars do TV now. Writers act in their own shows. And reality TV takes over prime time. In my personal life, my marriage ends. My kids graduate and start their careers. Too many people I love pass away.

You've Got Hate Mail brings us all around the globe. We win the Mexican equivalent of the Tony Award for Best Play. In Mexico City, people who find out who I am are quick to offer up their impressions of Sheneneh from *Martin* for me. You go, *Martin*.

And most important, my time off from TV brings me actress Teresa Ganzel. A blind date we were supposed to go on with each other in 1979 finally takes place two years after my marriage ends. And we haven't looked back since.

I find it's true. Not all stories go A to B to C. As I learned on *Anything But Love*, sometimes A to B to Q is better.

The run of the play ends, and Jane and I return to TV by selling a series of pilots. And, between plays, we're still at it.

People ask "why?" "Why do you keep doing this?" "You don't need the money." I admit it's an insane job. If you're lucky enough to sell a pilot, your reward is getting to do the same thing every week, in less time, for less money, with different groups of people telling you how you're doing it wrong the entire time.

Each time we take on a show, I hear my friends saying, "You don't need it!" But here's a secret: I do need it. I need the creative challenge of taking a blank sheet of paper and creating a new world. I need the pressure and the problem-solving and the thinking on your feet and the craziness of it all. I love making people laugh. It makes me feel alive. And there's nothing I like better than being in a Writers Room with funny people. It's there I've had some of the best laughs of my life.

So we keep at it. It's not like I have a choice. Every morning, I still wake up and head straight for the computer. And if I ever hesitate about taking a job or a meeting, Jane will always be here to tell me: "We're not done yet. Get in the car, Billy.

END CREDITS

TV SERIES

Anything But Love

Bless This House

Center of the Universe

Daddy Dearest

The Hughleys

Martin

Newhart

Nurses

Sydney

Ties That Bind

The Wayans Bros.

Yes, Dear

TV PILOTS

Alive & Kicking (Olympia Dukakis, Richard Mulligan)

Bebe From the Block (Cedric the Entertainer)

Bitter Women

Crossing Bridges (Tichina Arnold)

Daddy Dearest (Don Rickles, Richard Lewis)

Dalton & French

Elvis Has Left the Basement

Five Little Mulligans

Happy Together (Julia Duffy)

Heart & Soul
Jack and Janet Save the Planet
Jamie Lee Curtis Project (Jamie Lee Curtis)
Kids in Space
The Johnsons Are Home (Louie Anderson)
Marriage Sucks
Mommy, Daddy & Phil
My Little Town
New Amsterdam/Manna Hatta
People in Big Houses
Plan B
Reservations
The Sex is Always Greener
Starting Under
Staten Island 10309 (David Krumholz)
Suddenly Susan (Brooke Shields)
The Wayans Bros. (The Wayans Bros.)
Witless Protection
Young Barbarians

TV SPECIALS

I Love Lucy: The Very First Show (Emmy Nomination)

PLAYS

Bathroom Humor
The Boomer Boys
Confessions of a Dirty Blonde
Do Not Disturb
Drop Dead!
Firm Indecision
Having a Wonderful Time, Wish You Were Her

High School Reunion: The Musical
Infidelities
Lie, Cheat, and Genuflect
A Little Quickie
Love, Sex, and the I.R.S.
Merrily We Dance and Sing (The Naughty Boy)
A Night at the Nutcracker
The Pennies
Playing Doctor
The Property Known as Garland
The Senator Wore Pantyhose
Silent Laughter
Suitehearts
Till Death Do Us Part
What the Bellhop Saw
What the Rabbi Saw
Wrong Window
Young Barbarians